Department for Children, Schools and Families

The Children's Plan
Building brighter futures

Presented to Parliament
by the Secretary of State for Children, Schools and Families
by Command of Her Majesty

December 2007

Cm 7280

Table of Contents

Foreword

By the Secretary of State for Children, Schools and Families

Our aim is to make this the best place in the world for our children and young people to grow up. This is why we created the new Department for Children, Schools and Families six months ago, and why we announced that we would draw up this first ever Children's Plan, to put the needs of families, children and young people at the centre of everything we do.

Since then, we have been listening to parents, teachers, professionals, and children and young people themselves. We heard that while there are more opportunities for young people today than ever before, parents want more support in managing the new pressures they face such as balancing work and family life, dealing with the internet and the modern commercial world, and letting their children play and learn whilst staying safe. We heard that while children are doing better than ever in school, we need to do more to ensure that every child gets a world class education. We heard that while fewer children now live in poverty, too many children's education is still being held back by poverty and disadvantage.

And so building on a decade of reform and results, and responding directly to these concerns, our Children's Plan will strengthen support for all families during the formative early years of their children's lives, take the next steps in achieving world class schools and an excellent education for every child, involve parents fully in their children's learning, help to make sure that young people have interesting and exciting things to do outside of school, and provide more places for children to play safely.

The Plan and the new Department mean that more than ever before families will be at the centre of excellent, integrated services that put their needs first, regardless of traditional institutional and professional structures. This means a new leadership role for Children's Trusts in every area, a new role for schools as the centre of their communities, and more effective links between schools, the NHS and other children's services so that together they can engage parents and tackle all the barriers to the learning, health and happiness of every child.

I am also determined to make sure that this Children's Plan is the beginning of a new way of working, not a one-off event. As well as making sure that everyone understands what part they need to play, we need to carry on listening if we are going to get this right and help all our children and young people aim high and achieve their ambitions. There will also be an opportunity to feed in to the different reviews that we have announced.

We are setting ourselves ambitious new goals for 2020, and we will report back on the progress we are making on the Plan in a year's time. With schools, children's services, the voluntary sector and government all playing their part, we can ensure that every child has the best start in life, we can back all parents as they bring up their children, we can unlock the talents of all our young people and we can ensure that no child or young person is left to fall behind.

That is what our Children's Plan sets out to do.

Ed Balls
Secretary of State for Children, Schools and Families

Executive summary

1.   The Children's Plan aims to make England the best place in the world for children and young people to grow up. Over the last ten years, we have made much progress to tackle under investment and low aspirations in early years, schools, colleges and other services for children. Since 1997:

  - the number of registered childcare places has more than doubled so that there is now a registered childcare place for 1 in every 4 children under 8;

  - standards in schools have risen across the board, with results at ages 11, 14, 16 and 19 now at or about their highest ever levels, far fewer weak or failing schools, and more young people than ever before going on to university;

  - the number of children in relative poverty has fallen by 600,000 and teenage pregnancy rates are at their lowest level for 20 years; and

  - as a result of Every Child Matters, local areas have begun to change the way they manage their services for children and young people.

2.   However, while there are more opportunities for families and children now than ever before, parents say they sometimes find it hard to cope with a rapidly changing world. More mothers as well as fathers are pursuing rewarding careers, but can find it hard to balance work and family life. Parents regret that their children do not play independently outside as they did when they were young, but worry about safety if their children go outside alone. Families are more aware of how to pursue healthy lifestyles but too much time spent in front of video games or the television and fatty foods mean that child obesity is on the rise. And when this generation of children and young people leave education, they will need higher skills to succeed in employment.

3.   Moreover, some children and young people, often from disadvantaged backgrounds, are still underachieving. While many of our teachers and schools are among the very best in the world, there is still too much variation in quality, and as a result children are not achieving all of which they are capable. And too many children and young people suffer unhappy childhoods because of disadvantage or problems that are not addressed, or tackled too late.

4.   Based on our consultation, five principles underpin the Children's Plan:

  - government does not bring up children – parents do – so government needs to do more to back parents and families;

  - all children have the potential to succeed and should go as far as their talents can take them;

  - children and young people need to enjoy their childhood as well as grow up prepared for adult life;

- services need to be shaped by and responsive to children, young people and families, not designed around professional boundaries; and

- it is always better to prevent failure than tackle a crisis later.

5. The Children's Plan sets out our plans for the next ten years under each of the Department for Children, Schools and Families' strategic objectives, with a chapter at the end looking at how we will make these reforms happen.

Chapter 1: Happy and healthy

Secure the wellbeing and health of children and young people

6. Families are the bedrock of society and the place for nurturing happy, capable and resilient children. In our consultation, parents made it clear that they would like better and more flexible information and support that reflects the lives they lead. Our expert groups emphasised how important it is that parents are involved with policy affecting children and that we need particularly to improve how government and services involve fathers. To help every parent do the best for their child, we will:

    - allocate £34 million over the next three years to provide two expert parenting advisers in every local authority;

    - expand school-based Parent Support Advisers;

    - develop for parents a personal progress record on their child's development from the early years to primary school, building on the idea behind the 'red book' on young children's health; and

    - put parents' views at the heart of government by creating a new Parents Panel to advise us on policies affecting parents.

7. Some families need more intensive help than others and to ensure they receive that support we will:

    - ensure all families benefit from Sure Start Children's Centres by improving outreach services;

    - strengthen intensive support to the neediest families by piloting a key worker approach, bringing services together around need;

    - help families in which children are caring for others;

    - invest £90 million capital over three years to improve facilities for disabled children to take short breaks; and

    - extend the Family Fund which supports the families of disabled children by offering support up to age 18.

8. Parents and children told us that they wanted safe places to play outside, and we know that play has real benefits for children. We will spend £225 million over the next three years to:

    - offer every local authority capital funding that would allow up to 3,500 playgrounds nationally to be rebuilt or renewed and made accessible to children with disabilities;

- create 30 new adventure playgrounds for 8- to 13-year-olds in disadvantaged areas, supervised by trained staff; and

- we will publish a play strategy by summer 2008.

9. Good health is vital if children and young people are to enjoy their childhood and achieve their full potential. If we can establish good habits in childhood, this will provide the basis for lifelong health and wellbeing. To improve children's health we will:

    - publish a Child Health Strategy in spring 2008, produced jointly between the Department for Children, Schools and Families and the Department of Health; and

    - review Child and Adolescent Mental Health Services to see how universal, mainstream and specialist support services can be improved for the growing number of children and young people with mental health needs.

10. Poverty blights children's lives, which is why we have committed to halve child poverty by 2010 and eradicate it by 2020. The new joint Department for Children, Schools and Families and Department for Work and Pensions Child Poverty Unit will coordinate work across government to break the cycle of poverty from generation to generation. Poor housing is a particular problem for poor families and tackling it is important to meeting our 2020 goal and so we will:

    - tackle overcrowding, publishing an action plan in 2008; and

    - prioritise children's needs in housing decisions, especially the need to stay close to services like schools.

Chapter 2: Safe and Sound

Safeguard the young and vulnerable

11. Keeping children and young people safe from harm must be the priority and responsibility of us all. However, children need also to be able to learn, have new experiences and enjoy their childhoods, so we will help families strike the right balance between keeping children safe and allowing them the freedom they need. So we will:

    - publish Dr Tanya Byron's review on the potential risks to children from exposure to harmful or inappropriate content on the internet and in video games;

    - commission an independent assessment of the impact of the commercial world on children's wellbeing;

    - fund a new home safety equipment scheme to prevent the accidents which happen to young children in the home;

    - encourage local authorities to create 20mph zones, where appropriate, because they can reduce child pedestrian deaths by 70 per cent; and

    - strengthen the complaints procedure for parents whose children experience bullying.

12. Government also has a responsibility to put in place the right frameworks and systems for safeguarding children and young people, working in partnership with key national and local organisations and so we will:

   ● publish the *Staying Safe Action Plan* in early 2008, responding to the *Staying Safe* consultation; and

   ● ensure that schools and local authorities take a proportionate approach to health and safety to allow children to take risks while staying safe.

Chapter 3: Excellence and equity

Individual progress to achieve world class standards and close the gap in educational achievement for disadvantaged children

13. We want every young person to achieve their potential and enjoy their time in education. Parents' support for their child's learning is an essential foundation for achievement. Parents told us they want to be more involved in their children's education, and schools see the benefits of greater engagement with parents. High quality early years education ensures that children are ready to succeed at school and is particularly beneficial to those from disadvantaged backgrounds. Our Expert Groups told us that the best way to achieve world class standards is a system in which all children receive teaching tailored to their needs and which is based on their 'stage not age'.

14. Partnership with parents is a unifying theme of the Children's Plan. Early years settings, primary schools and the best secondary schools have done much to work with parents and involve them in their child's education. However, we have further to go to deliver our vision for all parents, especially in secondary school, and so:

   ● we will set out and consult on a new relationship between parents and schools and legislate if necessary in order that:
      – parents will be contacted by a staff member at secondary school before their child starts at the school;
      – parents will be able to attend information sessions at the new school;
      – every child will have a personal tutor who knows them in the round, and act as a main contact for parents;
      – parents will have regular, up to date information on their child's attendance behaviour and progress in learning;
      – Parents Councils will ensure that parents' voices are heard within the school; and
      – parents' complaints will be managed in a straightforward and open way

   ● we will spend £30 million over the next three years to provide more family learning to help parents and carers develop skills and learn with their children in schools.

15. Having created over the last decade a universal early years and childcare system, and having raised the entitlement to free early education and childcare for 3- and 4-year-olds from 12.5 to 15 hours a week, we will now invest £100 million over three years to:

   ● extend the offer of up to 15 hours of free early education and childcare to 20,000 2-year-olds in the most disadvantaged communities.

16. In schools, building on the £144 million already allocated over the next three years in the Every Child a Reader and Every Child Counts programmes to provide intensive support to children in primary schools at risk of falling behind, we will:

- allocate £25 million over the next three years to an Every Child a Writer programme to offer intensive one-to-one coaching in the areas of writing children find hardest to master;

- offer new 'age not stage' tests which children will take when they are ready and which, if current trials prove successful, will replace Key Stage tests at ages 11 and 14; and

- publish new indicators to show the performance of pupils achieving Level 7 or above in English, mathematics and science and achieving Level 8 and above in mathematics, to ensure proper attention is given to gifted and talented learners.

17. As our experts highlighted, the curriculum should help children move seamlessly from nurseries to schools, from primary to secondary and then to work or further and higher education. It should ensure all children secure the basics, while allowing flexibility to learn new skills and develop the social and emotional skills they need to succeed. Therefore we have announced a root and branch review of the primary curriculum, led by Sir Jim Rose, to ensure there is:

- more time for the basics so children achieve a good grounding in reading, writing and mathematics;

- greater flexibility for other subjects;

- time for primary school children to learn a modern foreign language; and

- a smoother transition from play-based learning in the early years into primary school, particularly to help summer-born children who can be at a disadvantage when they enter primary school.

18. In order to meet our 2020 goals for educational achievement, we will need to improve the attainment of some specific groups who we know are currently under performing. Our vision is that there will be ready access from schools to the range of support services necessary to ensure barriers to learning are broken down. We will:

- spend £18 million over the next three years to improve quality of teaching for children with special educational needs, including:
  - better initial teacher training and continuing professional development;
  - better data for schools on how well children with special educational needs are progressing; and
  - a pilot scheme in which children with dyslexia will receive Reading Recovery support or one-to-one tuition from specialist dyslexia teachers.

- ask Her Majesty's Chief Inspector of Schools to review progress on special educational needs in 2009, in the light of the impact of greater personalised learning.

Chapter 4: Leadership and collaboration

System reform to achieve world class standards and close the gap in educational achievement for disadvantaged children

19. If we are to achieve the potential improvement in standards from personalisation, we need to create an early years and schools system where all institutions are consistently achieving at the level of the best.

20. The single most important factor in delivering our aspirations for children is a world class workforce able to provide highly personalised support, so we will continue to drive up quality and capacity of those working in the children's workforce. We know from our consultation how important the quality of early years childcare and education is to improving children's achievement. So we will invest £117 million over the next three years in the early years workforce, including measures to:

   - fund supply cover so early years workers can take part in continuing professional development; and

   - boost the Graduate Leader Fund so that every full daycare setting will be led by a graduate by 2015, with two graduates per setting in disadvantaged areas.

21. We already have many teachers and headteachers who are among the best in the world. However, to deliver a teaching workforce and a new generation of headteachers which is consistently world class we will allocate £44 million over the next three years to:

   - make teaching a Masters level profession by working with the social partnership to introduce a new qualification, building on the recently agreed performance management measures;

   - ensure new recruits spend at least one year in training;

   - establish a Transition to Teaching programme to attract more people with science, technology and engineering backgrounds into teaching; and

   - extend the Future Leaders programme which places people with proven leadership credentials into urban schools.

22. By promoting diversity in a collaborative system we can ensure that children, young people and parents are able to choose provision that reflects their particular needs. Schools and other settings can use their increased freedoms to innovate and find new solutions to problems, which can then be shared with others to ensure all children benefit. To strengthen both diversity and collaboration, we are expecting every secondary school to have specialist, trust or academy status and every school to have a business or university partner, with 230 academies by 2010 on the road to 400. Through strengthened accountability and governance, we will build on the successes of the last ten years in reducing the number of failing schools. We expect local authorities to take swift and decisive action to prevent schools from failing and to reverse failure quickly when it happens. We also expect local authorities actively to challenge schools who are not improving their pupils' performance but are coasting. We have already set a goal that within five years no secondary school should have fewer than 30 per cent of pupils gaining 5 higher level GCSEs. To improve the

quality of accountability and governance and in addition to our measures to strengthen parental engagement in schools we will:

- make governing bodies more effective, beginning by consulting on reducing the size of governing bodies.

Chapter 7 sets out further detail on how we expect schools to work together and with other services to break down barriers to learning

23. We know that standards of behaviour continue to be a matter of concern for parents, teachers, and children and young people themselves. It is important that the environment in every classroom supports effective teaching and learning and we have made it easier for teachers to enforce discipline and good behaviour. We currently expect secondary schools to be in behaviour partnerships, as recommended in Sir Alan Steer's 2005 report, to work together to improve behaviour and tackle persistent absence as well as improve outcomes for those whose behaviour is poor. Sir Alan's report recommended that participation in behaviour partnerships should be compulsory from 2008. Given that 97 per cent of schools are already participating, we are minded to implement this recommendation and will:

- ask Sir Alan Steer to review progress since his report and the effectiveness of behaviour partnerships; and

- depending on his findings make participation in them compulsory for all maintained schools and all new academies, encouraging all existing academies to take part as well.

24. Children who behave poorly and are excluded, those unable to attend a mainstream school and those disengaged from education are a relatively small proportion of pupils. However, they include some of the young people with the worst prospects for success in later life, and most likely to develop problem behaviours. The quality of education they receive is highly variable despite the difference it can make to their prospects. To address this we will:

- spend £26.5 million over the next three years on piloting new forms of alternative provision which could include using small schools – studio schools – with close links to business and providing a high quality vocational education; and

- ask local authorities to collect and publish performance data for pupils not on a school roll, to ensure local areas have incentives to improve their performance.

25. To deliver world class education and children's services we need world class buildings and use of technology. We will continue with our unprecedented investment in the fabric of schools and children and young people's services to create schools fit for the 21st century and will:

- produce guidance within the Building Schools for the Future programme to ensure that where possible new buildings make space for co-located services; and

- set an ambition for all new school buildings to be zero carbon by 2016. We know that with the technologies currently available, the zero carbon ambition cannot be achieved on many school sites. We are therefore appointing a taskforce to advise on how to achieve zero carbon schools, whether the timescale is realistic and how to reduce carbon emissions in the intervening period.

Chapter 5: Staying on

Ensure that young people are participating and achieving their potential to 18 and beyond

26. A changing economy means we need to ensure our children and young people have the right skills as they become adults and move into further or higher education, or into work. By 2015, we want all young people to stay on in education or training to 18 and beyond. And when they leave we want them to have the skills they need to prosper in a high skills economy.

27. To achieve this we must reduce the numbers who are not in education, employment and training. Diplomas and Apprenticeships will increase the learning options available to 14–19-year-olds and will also help tackle the concerns raised by employers and higher education institutes about the broader functional and personal, learning and thinking skills of learners. To reinforce the impact of 14–19 reform, we will:

    - legislate in this Parliamentary session to raise the participation age to 17 from 2013 and 18 from 2015;

    - develop 3 new Diplomas in science, humanities and languages to increase the options for young people;

    - create a new independent regulator of qualifications, with the consultation launched before the end of 2007;

    - transfer funding for 16–19 learning from the Learning and Skills Council to local authorities, with a consultation on how best to achieve this in early 2008; and

    - allocate £31.5 million over the next three years on a new programme to re-engage 16-year-olds who are not currently engaged in learning, building on the extra measures we have announced on NEETs, including better tracking and financial incentives to remain in learning.

Chapter 6: On the right track

Keeping children and young people on the path to success

28. We want all young people to enjoy happy, healthy and safe teenage years and to be prepared for adult life. Too often we focus on the problems of a few young people rather than the successes of the many – we want a society where young people feel valued and in which their achievements are recognised and celebrated.

29. Positive activities and experiences are a vital part of happy and enjoyable teenage years. We have established a Youth Task Force to ensure that we improve delivery of young people's services and so that they are designed around their needs. We have already announced investment of £60 million in improving youth facilities in advance of funding released from unclaimed assets. But we want further and faster transformation of the lives of young people and so we will:

    - invest £160 million over the next two years to improve the quality and range of places for young people to go and things for them to do;

- develop an entitlement for all young people to participate in positive activities which develop their talents including piloting a new offer to take part in cultural activities in and out of school; and

- spend £20 million over the next three years to use Acceptable Behaviour Contracts as a measure to prevent young people engaging in antisocial behaviour and to ensure young people receive support to improve their behaviour at the same time as an Antisocial Behaviour Order.

30. Experimentation in early teenage years and adolescence can expose young people to risks, and where they fail to make informed and sensible choices, they can too often put their health and future at stake. To tackle behaviour that puts young people at risk and help young people manage these risks, we will:

- publish a youth alcohol action plan in spring 2008, around the same time as the new Drugs Strategy which will:
    - improve alcohol education in schools;
    - tackle parental alcohol misuse which can influence young people's own consumption; and
    - consider the case for further action on alcohol advertising.

31. Following Expert Group discussions of the importance of relationships as young people move from adolescence to adulthood we will:

- review best practice in effective sex and relationships education and how it is delivered in schools.

32. The majority of young people do not offend but we need to reduce the harm caused by youth crime both to those who are victims and to young offenders themselves. In advance of the Youth Crime Action Plan, the Children's Plan sets out how we want mainstream services to work together to prevent crime, what we will do to deal swiftly with those involved in youth crime and how we will prevent reoffending including:

- allocating, with the Home Office, £66 million over the next three years to target those most at risk;

- piloting a restorative approach to youth offenders; and

- publishing a Green Paper in 2008 looking at what happens when young offenders leave custody and consult on how to improve the education they receive in custody.

Chapter 7: Making it happen

Vision for 21st century children's services

33. Delivering the vision set out in the Children's Plan will require a series of system-wide reforms to the way services for children and young people work together. By putting the needs of children and families first, we will provide a service that makes more sense to the parents, children and young people using them, for whom professional boundaries can appear arbitrary and frustrating. By locating services under one roof in the places people visit frequently, they are more likely to find the help they need. And by investing in all of those who work with children, and by building capacity to work across professional boundaries we can ensure that joining up services is not just about providing a safety net for the vulnerable – it is about unlocking the potential of every child.

34. We want to build on the ambitions set out in Every Child Matters, and deliver a step change in outcomes. We will:

- expect every school to be uncompromising in its ambitions for achievement, sitting at the heart of the community it serves;

- set high expectations for Children's Trusts to:
  - deliver measurable improvements for all children and young people;
  - have in place by 2010 consistent, high quality arrangements to provide identification and early intervention for all children and young people who need additional help;

- monitor the difference Children's Trusts are making and examine whether Children's Trust arrangements need to be strengthened to improve outcomes, including by further legislation; and

- publish a Children's Workforce Action Plan in early 2008, covering everyone who works with children and young people, which will strengthen integrated working across all services.

Goals for 2020

35. The Children's Plan also sets out goals we have for what we can and should achieve for our children by 2020. These should be aspirational for both children and young people's educational attainment and for their wider wellbeing. We will consult widely over the next year on whether these goals represent the right national ambitions:

- enhance children and young people's wellbeing, particularly at key transition points in their lives;

- every child ready for success in school, with at least 90 per cent developing well across all areas of the Early Years Foundation Stage Profile by age 5;

- every child ready for secondary school, with at least 90 per cent achieving at or above the expected level in both English and mathematics by age 11;

- every young person with the skills for adult life and further study, with at least 90 per cent achieving the equivalent of five higher level GCSEs by age 19; and at least 70 per cent achieving the equivalent of two A levels by age 19;

- parents satisfied with the information and support they receive;

- all young people participating in positive activities to develop personal and social skills, promote wellbeing and reduce behaviour that puts them at risk;

- employers satisfied with young people's readiness for work;

- child health improved, with the proportion of obese and overweight children reduced to 2000 levels;

- child poverty halved by 2010 and eradicated by 2020; and

- significantly reduce by 2020 the number of young offenders receiving a conviction, reprimand, or final warning for a recordable offence for the first time, with a goal to be set in the Youth Crime Action Plan.

36. We will report on progress in delivering the Children's Plan in a year's time.

Introduction

1. The Children's Plan sets out our ambitions for improving children and young people's lives over the next decade and how we intend to achieve them. By 2020 we want England to be the best place in the world to grow up. Despite the progress we have made in the last ten years, achieving this will require new commitment over the long term and across all areas of Government policy.

2. The creation of the new Department for Children, Schools and Families (DCSF) represents the first time Government has focused exclusively on issues affecting children and young people. The Department works across Government to make sure that all the aspects of children's lives are taken into account and prioritised.

3. Parents bring up children, not governments, and we want this Children's Plan to mark the beginning of a new kind of relationship in which the Government commits to working in close partnership with families at every level, from making policy to delivering services. In this spirit, in drawing up this Children's Plan we started by asking children, young people, parents, professionals and employers about what our priorities should be – about what they value, what worries them, and what we could do better.

4. We held events across the country at which parents and professionals debated the issues affecting children and young people. We invited children and young people to participate in discussion and held an online consultation to gather views. We also established three groups of experts to advise us on how we should deliver our priorities, looking at 0–7s, 8–13s and 14–19s. More information about how the consultation took place is included at Annex A.

5. The results of the consultation and the recommendations of the Expert Groups have guided the development of the Children's Plan. Because we value children as young citizens, we have developed the Plan with regard to the principles and articles of the UN Convention on the Rights of the Child. Annex B shows how the content of the Children's Plan reflects and is informed by the Convention.

6. The Department for Children, Schools and Families has six strategic objectives to improve children and young people's lives:

   - secure the health and wellbeing of children and young people;
   - safeguard the young and vulnerable;
   - achieve world-class standards;
   - close the gap in educational achievement for children from disadvantaged backgrounds;
   - ensure young people are participating and achieving their potential to 18 and beyond; and
   - keep children and young people on the path to success.

7.	The Children's Plan sets out what we are doing to achieve each of these strategic objectives. Each chapter of the plan covers a strategic objective except for Chapters 3 and 4. Because our strategies for world class standards and for closing the gap in educational achievement are so closely bound together and cannot be seen as alternatives, Chapter 3 sets out how we will work to ensure every child makes progress and then Chapter 4 looks at how we will build an excellent system to deliver our reforms.

8.	Achieving our ambition is dependent on all services for children working together at a local level. Chapter 7 sets out our vision for a children's services system in the 21st century – with schools at its heart and a highly skilled children's workforce working in concert to improve children's lives. Throughout the text, we have marked in bold where we have recently announced a new policy or approach or where we are setting out new commitments in the Children's Plan.

9.	Because we do not see the Plan as an end but as the beginning of new engagement between Government and children, families and experts, Annex C sets out the next steps. This includes our intention to continue to consult children and parents about their concerns and to continue to ask our Expert Groups to advise us on what action we should be taking. In a year, we will publish a report of our progress.

Chapter 1: Happy and healthy

Secure the wellbeing and health of children and young people

Executive summary

1.1 Families are the bedrock of society and the place for nurturing happy, capable and resilient children. In our consultation, parents made it clear that they would like better and more flexible information and support that reflects the lives they lead. Our expert groups emphasised how important it is that parents are involved with policy affecting children and that we need particularly to improve how government and services involve fathers. To help every parent do the best for their child, we will:

- allocate £34 million over the next three years to provide two expert parenting advisers in every local authority;

- expand school-based Parent Support Advisers;

- develop for parents a personal progress record on their child's development from the early years to primary school, building on the idea behind the 'red book' on young children's health; and

- put parents' views at the heart of government by creating a new Parents Panel to advise us on policies affecting parents.

1.2 Some families need more intensive help than others and to ensure they receive that support we will:

- ensure all families benefit from Sure Start Children's Centres by improving outreach services;

- strengthen intensive support to the neediest families by piloting a key worker approach, bringing services together around need;

- help families in which children are caring for others;

- make £90 million capital investment to improve facilities for disabled children to take short breaks; and

- extend the Family Fund which supports the families of disabled children by extending support to age 18.

1.3   Parents and children told us that they wanted safe places to play outside and we know that play has real benefits for children. We will spend £225 million over the three years to 2010–11 to:

- offer every local authority capital funding that would allow up to 3,500 playgrounds nationally to be rebuilt or renewed and made accessible to children with disabilities;

- create 30 new adventure playgrounds for 8- to 13-year-olds in disadvantaged areas, supervised by trained staff; and

- publish a play strategy by summer 2008.

1.4   Good health is vital if children and young people are to enjoy their childhood and achieve their full potential. If we can establish good habits in childhood, this will provide the basis for lifelong health and wellbeing. To improve children's health we will:

- publish a Child Health Strategy in spring 2008, produced jointly between Department for Children, Schools and Families and the Department of Health; and

- review Children and Adolescent Mental Health Services to see how universal, mainstream and specialist support services can be improved for the growing number of children and young people with mental health needs.

1.5   Poverty blights children's lives, which is why we have committed to halve child poverty by 2010 and eradicate it by 2020. The new joint Department for Children, Schools and Families and Department for Work and Pensions Child Poverty Unit will coordinate work across government to break the cycle of poverty from generation to generation. Poor housing is a particular problem for poor families and tackling it is important to meeting our 2020 goal and so we will:

- tackle overcrowding, publishing an action plan in 2008; and

- prioritise children's needs in housing decisions, especially the need to stay close to services like schools.

Vision for the next decade

1.6   No one can guarantee wellbeing and health for every child, but as a society it must be our aspiration for children and young people to have a good childhood, and live free from the avoidable causes of poor health and unhappiness. We want to see each child and young person feeling well prepared for the next phase of growing up at each stage of their journey to adulthood. Our priority is to ensure every child enjoys the benefits of living in strong and stable families, with an active and healthy lifestyle.

1.7   The Government has set out its commitment to improving the health and wellbeing of children and young people over the next three years in a new Public Service Agreement (Improve the health and wellbeing of children and young people, PSA 12). The PSA takes forward the vision for delivering the standards for high quality child-centred health services set out in the National Service Framework for Children, Young People and Maternity Services. This PSA will drive these priorities through the following indicators:

- prevalence of breastfeeding at 6–8 weeks;

- percentage of pupils who have school lunches;

- levels of child obesity;

- emotional health and wellbeing, and Child and Adolescent Mental Health Services (CAMHS); and

- parents' experience of services for disabled children.

1.8 By 2020 we want to see:

- families able to achieve all their ambitions for their children, knowing where to find the support and information they need and treated as partners whenever they engage with professionals;

- children able to grow up free of the blight of child poverty, with child poverty halved by 2010 and eradicated by 2020;

- children enjoying healthy lifestyles and outcomes, with the proportion of overweight and obese children back to year 2000 levels, and with excellent services for children and young people with physical and mental health problems;

- all children with the social and emotional capabilities that they will need for a successful adult life; and

- all children able to enjoy an active childhood, with safe places to play independently.

A family policy for the 21st century

1.9 A modern family policy starts from what helps family life to flourish. Our vision is of all families being confident in their ability to achieve the best for their child. Parents and carers expect to be responsible for every aspect of their child's development, prepared to trust the judgement of professionals, who consult and engage them on the way. They want information, advice and support to be easily accessible and available when they need it.

1.10 Different families will need different things at different times and in different circumstances. The challenge is to provide services which are flexible and meet the needs of all families, in whatever shape or form. Our family policy will support families with whatever level of information and support they need, when they need it. This will include lone parent families, step families, and families where children are being brought up by their grandparents.

1.11 This means recognising that life is more complex than it ever was. Employment patterns are changing, and more women than ever and an increasing number of men too are juggling family life with paid work. More parents are providing support and care to elderly relatives as well as bringing up children. We want to encourage and support fathers so that they can play a bigger role in their children's lives, both at home and in school. Some fathers bring up children on their own, and we will ensure that services are responsive to the particular issues they face.

1.12 Over the last decade, services for families have changed enormously. Many more families are now getting the information, advice and, when necessary, the help they need thanks to Sure Start Children's Centres and extended schools; responsibilities on local authorities to provide access to advice and support; and specialist support for families who need most help through Parent Support Advisers, Nurse Family Partnerships and Family Intervention Projects. But there is some way to go to provide properly family-centred public services.

1.13 We will ensure all public services act to help families help themselves. We need to make it easier for mothers and fathers to support their child's health development by giving them better information, when and where they need it, and by making it easier to navigate services. As we show in Chapter 3, we are committed to strengthening the relationship between parents and schools. We also need to reach out to the minority of families who most need help but do not always come forward without additional encouragement and support.

Informing and involving parents

1.14 Many parents report experiencing practical problems getting the help they need, and mainstream services are not always organised in a way that makes sense to them and is easy to access. Fathers, in particular, say that they often feel invisible to health and children's services professionals and find that many services are not offered at times that fit with their working patterns. Some ethnic groups are less inclined to make use of support that is available, and the same is true for disadvantaged families.

1.15 Local authorities, in particular through their Children's Information Services, play a vital part in informing parents of the support available in their area. To support local authorities in improving the availability of information and help for parents, we are developing a national telephone helpline service, Parent Know-How, and also a search engine to link available directories of services for parents. We are exploring the scope to provide information and advice through text and instant messaging, as well as using online social networking to provide parent-to-parent support.

1.16 Parents need to be confident about the standards and provision they have a right to expect, and their right to be involved in shaping services and demanding improvements. We are currently developing a Parents' Charter, which will describe the minimum level of support all parents can expect to receive from their local authority. All local children's services, will offer their own Parents' Charter, which will set out what parents are entitled to at each stage of their children's lives.

1.17 Parents need timely and meaningful information about their child's development and needs so they can help them to flourish. Taking forward a proposal made by the Expert Groups, we will look to extend the principle behind the 'red book' given to every parent to track their child's health development through the first years of its life by exploring how we can develop a **personal parent-held record that will run from birth to age 11**, and potentially beyond. We will also look at how schools can use online information to let parents know how their children are developing, coupled with advice on how they can support them further. Improved and more regular detail about their child's performance promised by 'real-time reporting' in schools (set out in Chapter 3) will be an important element.

> "[I would like] to know where to get help and advice and access it promptly, be aware of health issues, ensure children are aware of healthy lifestyle issues." (Parent, Paper survey)

> "The government could make some sort of fact sheet of everything that is available to parents/carers or put something online or maybe a telephone helpline that parents could phone and be given all the information that they need." (Online survey)

1.18 Services for families are always more effective when they have been closely involved in their design and development. Some local authorities have developed effective mechanisms for seeking families' views about services. We expect to see forums in all areas for parents of disabled children so that they can participate in shaping local services. **To provide a voice for parents at the heart of government, we will set up a new national Parents' Panel with links into a full cross-section of parental opinion, so these perspectives are better reflected in government policy making.** In addition, we will measure the confidence and satisfaction of parents in the services they use.

Reaching the most vulnerable families

> *"I would improve moral support for families in need to let them know that they are supported." (Young person, Paper survey)*

1.19 Parents who for whatever reason lack the confidence, motivation or time to get involved with their child's learning and development may need extra specialist help. These are often families who have suffered from generations of disadvantage, whose children stand to benefit most from high quality early years provision and other help. Effective home visiting outreach and other outreach services can make a real difference to families who cannot or choose not to access services, providing important information and access to services such as childcare and family support. We announced earlier in 2007 that we will **expand outreach so that there are a minimum of two outreach workers in Sure Start Children's Centres in the most disadvantaged areas**.

Case study: Parent-to-parent support

Manchester City Council encourages parents who have attended parenting support sessions to go on to mentor other parents. This involves befriending other parents and encouraging them to attend by reminding them about dates and accompanying them to sessions. The work has proved very successful in ensuring that parents who are unlikely to attend groups on their own do attend and benefit.

Attending parenting groups can also help parents develop the skills and confidence they need to return to work. L, a parent of two, attended a 12 week Incredible Years parenting group. Afterwards she joined the local parent forum which supports families who have completed parenting support. In the forum, parents discuss things they are struggling with and advise each other on how to respond based on the techniques they have learnt in the formal sessions.

L successfully applied for a post as a part-time parent support worker to the forum. Her role involves providing ongoing support to parents through home visits to discuss how the parent is putting the theory into practice and reinforcing what has been learnt on the programme as well as finding out what parents want from the forum and organising family activities. L feels she gained an enormous amount from taking the parenting course and without this she would not have had the confidence to apply for the support worker post.

1.20 1,200 schools are now using Parent Support Advisers to work with parents to improve children's behaviour and school attendance, offer advice with parenting, and provide support for children and parents at the first sign the child or young person may be experiencing social, health or behavioural issues. We have recently announced funding **to expand the availability of Parent Support Advisers, allowing them to reach 10–15 schools in each local authority**.

> *"Parents who are less well-informed and lack confidence should be offered support themselves delivered in a way which does not patronise them, or make them feel inadequate as parents."* (Parent, Online survey)

> *"…if they are having problems managing their children's behaviour, [parents should] be able to access support without the fear of social services taking their children into care, but providing advice, support and resources."* (Practitioner, London)

1.21 To provide support for families who are finding it hard to deal with their child's behaviour, **we will allocate £34 million over the next three years to provide two expert parenting advisers in every local authority**. These experts will build on the current network of Respect parenting experts, and will work through extended schools and across the local authority. They will support parents in helping each other, which we know from our consultation and Expert Groups is both popular and effective.

1.22 As we work with Sure Start Children's Centres, schools and local authorities to develop this approach we will invest in the **development of outreach services in Sure Start Children's Centres to ensure all families benefit.** We will establish core principles and standards for an effective and comprehensive outreach service and ensure it meets the diverse needs of different families and communities. We will support this with appropriate training materials and courses and provide additional funding for practitioners without other sources of funding, potentially enabling some 5,000 practitioners to take up new training opportunities.

Box 1.1: Engaging fathers

"My dad has helped me the most, in Year 7 I had loads of trouble and I didn't want to go into school, but he encouraged me and supported me loads." (Young girl, Liverpool)

We know that children benefit enormously from having strong relationships with their fathers, yet public services routinely fail to engage with fathers, particularly when the father does not live with the child. We will work with the Children's Workforce Development Council and the new National Academy for Parenting Practitioners to ensure that occupational standards and training for the workforce will reflect the need for **public services to engage with both father and mother except where there is a clear risk to the child to do so**.

As we move towards offering more regular up-to-date information on a child's progress (set out in Chapter 3) we will expect schools to keep contact details of all parents living apart from their children, to involve them where possible, and to identify and use best practice in engaging fathers.

In developing Parent Know-How we are taking account of ways in which information can be made more easily accessible for fathers, mindful of research which shows that 63 per cent of fathers say that their preferred channel for information and support is the internet.

As we increase outreach through Sure Start Children's Centres we will look to engage fathers, offering them support in strengthening their parenting skills.

1.23   Some families with complex needs are not ready to participate in group-based family support. We know that for some parents intensive support over the telephone over a number of weeks from a trained parenting expert can provide the support they need to start to resolved their issues and encourage them to access other local services and sources of help. **We will pilot an expansion of intensive phone-based support services – with the aim of reaching up to 10,000 parents over three years**.

1.24   Children's and adult services need to work closely together: this is particularly important for the families in greatest need of support. **We will strengthen intensive support to the neediest families by piloting a key worker approach.** An additional £13 million to support families with multiple problems was announced early in 2007. Taking forward proposals in the Government's Families At Risk Review, *Think Family*, we will deliver this support through 12–15 new Family Pathfinders, which build on the existing Family Intervention Project model. A dedicated key worker will conduct an assessment and co-ordinate the services the family needs. A contract between the family, key worker and agencies will make the commitment of all parties clear.

Supporting stability and coping with breakdown

1.25   An effective family policy must start with supporting strong couple relationships and stable, positive relationships within families. Good local services are important in helping families cope with the inevitable stresses and strains, in meeting their needs and giving them the opportunity to achieve a good quality of life. In addition, there are times in the normal course of events for every family when the demands on parents can be especially acute and lead to tension in their relationship.

1.26   It is important that services can recognise and support people through those periods of instability. For example, health visitors through the One Plus One programme are being trained to learn to listen to parents, spot problems between them following the birth of a baby, and offer specific help to the couple as well as ensuring the healthy development of the child. Settings such as Sure Start Children's Centres are signposting parents to relationship support if they need it; professionals working with teenagers at risk need to be able to see when a young person's behaviour is adding to the strain on the parents' relationship; and the parent and family services now developing in many schools will also be routes through which support can be offered.

1.27   However, a significant minority of children will experience family breakdown. While children do not in general see different family structures as a particular problem, with 70 per cent saying one parent can raise a family as well as two, conflict between parents and the instability and trauma during and after break-up can have a strongly negative impact on child wellbeing and affect long-term life chances. So the support the parents and the wider family, including grandparents, can provide for the child during family break-up is critical to that child's wellbeing and success.

1.28   Working across government and with organisations such as Cafcass **we will launch work on how better to support parents (including non-resident parents) and their children during and after family breakdown**. We will look to highlight opportunities for universal services to spot warning signs of relationship breakdown early and to signpost support to parents and children at critical moments. And we will look to find better ways to enable children to maintain regular contact with both parents if they part. As the period following birth can be a time of particular stress, we will ensure that outreach workers from Sure Start Children's Centres receive training to give them the confidence to support relationships at this time – listening without becoming overwhelmed, offering effective support and encouraging parents to seek their own solutions.

"When my parents split up we had counsellors asking us what we wanted to do – yeah it helped as sometimes you don't want to go straight to them [parents]." (Young boy, Plymouth)

Box 1.2: Reforming the child maintenance system

The Government is creating a new and more effective child maintenance system that is focused on tackling child poverty. The Child Maintenance and Enforcement Commission (C-MEC) will take on a wider role than ever before, by encouraging and supporting parents to make arrangements which suit them best – either between themselves or through the new statutory maintenance service. A key part of the reforms will be the creation of a new Information and Support Service for parents. Parents going through separation have to deal with an array of issues. Therefore the Department for Work and Pensions is working closely with other government departments and third sector organisations to ensure the new service has effective links to existing support services for parents. We expect that the full reform programme will lift a further 100,000 children out of poverty.

Children in care and on the edge of care

1.29 Children in care are among the most vulnerable children in the country. The White Paper *Care Matters: Time for Change* (2007) set out how we will improve support for families with children in care and on the edge of care, including new interventions for parents of adolescents who are offending or committing antisocial behaviour. We will require that relatives and friends are considered as potential carers as part of a child's care plan, and expect local authorities to work with birth parents while a child is in care to support an early and safe return home for the child or young person where appropriate.

1.30 We will work with local authorities to ensure that those in care for a significant period of their childhood benefit from additional stability in already disrupted lives by reducing the numbers of children who move placement too often. The Fostering Changes training programme will improve the parenting skills of foster carers, as well as ensuring that the emotional wellbeing of children in care is considered more routinely.

1.31 *Care Matters* also set out how we will improve the quality of 'corporate parenting' for those who are in care by strengthening the voice of the child and the role of the local authority, with a key role for both the Lead Member and the Director of Children's Services. In 2008 we will publish further detail on the implementation of *Care Matters*.

1.32 An estimated 45 per cent of children and young people in care have an identifiable mental health problem. We will monitor, through a new local government National Indicator Set, improvements in the mental health and emotional wellbeing of children in care. We will issue statutory guidance for health services and local authorities setting out how they should improve the health of children in care, including their mental health.

Young carers

1.33 Young carers are children under 18 who are providing substantial personal and/or emotional care to another family member who is affected by illness, disability or substance misuse. Typically, a young carer will be a young person providing care to a lone parent, often their mother, who may be either physically disabled or experiencing mental health problems. Young carers often feel their caring role is vital and want to continue to help in their families. However, many young people tell us that they feel that they are missing out on their education and other opportunities and are isolated from their peers.

1.34 Services should adopt a whole family approach. This means that children's and adult services must have arrangements in place to ensure that no young person's life is unnecessarily restricted because they are providing significant care to an adult with an identifiable community care need.

1.35 We will set out our plans to support young carers once the review of the Department of Health's Carers Strategy has concluded. However, to secure early progress, **we propose to build on existing plans for Family Pathfinders, extending them to model more effective, preventative support around families affected by illness, disability or substance misuse, who rely on the care of a child.**

Unaccompanied asylum seeking children

1.36 We appreciate the potential vulnerability of unaccompanied children, and the distress they may experience while waiting for a decision on their asylum claim without the support of a family. Government recognises that unaccompanied asylum-seeking children (UASC) are first and foremost children. Many unaccompanied asylum seekers will be supported as children in care by local authorities as, by definition, they enter the country without an adult to take parental responsibility for them and, therefore, the local authority will be responsible for assessing these young people's needs and supporting them to access services. These young people, as children in care, will benefit from the reforms that we are introducing in our Children and Young Persons Bill.

1.37 The Home Office Borders and Immigration Agency will set out their plans for improving support to USAC in their response to their consultation paper *Planning Better Outcomes and Support for Unaccompanied Asylum Seeking Children*. This will set out proposals for strengthening identification and support for trafficked children; and for improving the quality and timeliness of asylum decision making to reduce the uncertainty faced by UASC, so that planning for their care can support their integration or their safe return to their country of origin.

Disabled children

1.38 *Aiming high for disabled children: better support for families* set out our strategy for improving the lives of disabled children and their families. Backed by £340 million over the next three years from the Department for Children, Schools and Families (DCSF), with additional resources to be announced from the Department of Health (DH), the ambition is for a transformation in services for families with disabled children by 2011 by:

- improved short breaks provision for severely disabled children and their families through new investment and an expectation that all local authorities provide a short break full service offer;

- more accessible childcare, so that disabled children can benefit from early education and parents have improved opportunities to work;

- a Transition Support Programme, which will help disabled young people move into adulthood, with increased opportunities for education, employment and independent living;

- parents' forums in all areas shaping local services for disabled children; and

- individual budget pilots for families with disabled children.

1.39 **To improve facilities, we will invest £90 million over the next three years in short break provision. This funding for public, private and voluntary sector providers will help improve equipment, transport and facilities and allow more inclusive breaks, where severely disabled young people can take part in activities with their non-disabled peers.**

1.40 We have also made a commitment to review how services for families with disabled children are delivered and held accountable, putting the voice of parents at the heart of this process. We will work with local authorities and Primary Care Trusts to provide better information, increased transparency, more common assessment and improved participation and feedback on the services that are delivered. In addition, we have introduced a new Public Service Agreement indicator which is based on what parents tell us about the services they receive. In 2008–09 we will conduct the first annual survey of parents with disabled children to support the disability indicator.

1.41 Families with severely disabled children who are on low incomes face particular challenges, and often need tailored financial support to cope with the burden of serious and life-threatening health conditions on top of the support they receive from benefits and tax credits. The DCSF, with the devolved administrations, provides core funding to the UK-wide Family Fund. The Fund distributed 38,857 grants to low income families with severely disabled children in England in 2006–07 – averaging £549 per grant. Currently, only families with children under 16 are able to apply for the grant. However, we know that families with severely disabled young people aged 16 and 17 also need additional financial support. **With additional investment over the next three years, we want the Family Fund to increase the age threshold to 18.** This will provide up to 16,200 grants to enable disabled young people to make the transition to adulthood.

Adoption

1.42 The Adoption and Children Act 2002 modernised the legal framework for adoption, widening the pool of potential parents and ensuring that a wide range of support services are available so that more vulnerable children have the chance to live in a stable and loving family. Special guardianship orders, introduced by the 2002 Act, provide permanence for children who cannot return to their families, but for whom adoption is not the most suitable option. A special guardian is able to exercise parental responsibility to the exclusion of all others (in all but a small number of circumstances). Special guardianship also provides an entitlement to a wide range of support services.

1.43 In future, we want more children to achieve stability more quickly, and we are encouraging local authorities to reflect on the range of options available in planning for individual children. We plan further training to support the implementation of the 2002 Act, which will have a particular focus on special guardianship.

The children's social care workforce

1.44 As we move to a world class children's workforce we will develop the capacity and skills in the children's social care workforce. Building on *Options for Excellence* and *Care Matters* we will address turnover, quality of supervision and burnout of new children's social workers **and will pilot a newly qualified status from 2008–9 offering a year of guaranteed induction support as well as introducing quality standards and assessment.** We will expand entry routes into children's social work by **developing and piloting a fast-track work-based route into children's social work aimed at mature graduates.** And we will embark on a major, national, targeted marketing and communications campaign to encourage more people, and people from a wider range of professional backgrounds, to consider entering children's social work. We will announce in the forthcoming Children's Workforce Action Plan proposals to tackle recruitment and retention and to accelerate the pace of workforce remodelling in social care.

1.45 We want to improve initial training and continuing professional development for children's social workers to ensure that all have qualifications and skills that are fit for purpose. As a first step we will review the mechanisms for funding and delivering this training, including the need for legislative and regulatory changes. We will **establish a framework for professional development** to set out the standards and competences expected at different career stages, provide a coherent career pathway, and provide incentives for good social workers to remain on the front line. We will also explore how social pedagogy could be applied in this framework. We will say more about these proposals in the Children's Workforce Action Plan, which will be published early in 2008.

Active childhood

1.46 Children want places to play, and parents want their children to enjoy the same freedoms they had when they were growing up. But they feel there are few attractive places for them to go and they worry about their safety. Supervised and unsupervised outdoor activities are important for children's development and also to reduce obesity, build social and emotional resilience, develop social skills, strengthen friendships, help children learn how to deal with risks – and of course because children enjoy them. However children spend less time in outdoor activities than they want to and than their own parents did as children. We will work with communities to create new and safer places to play and safe routes to play areas, and to provide positive structured activities for younger children.

> *"We need parks with park-keepers, leisure and adventure sports facilities, places where young, old, teenagers and families can all mingle and have fun." (Parents, Online survey)*

Play

1.47 The legal protection of school playing fields, introduced in 1998, has ensured that there are facilities for this and future generations. By opening facilities for longer hours, extended schools are maximising the use of playing fields and providing greater opportunities for children and young people, including disabled children, to take part in a wide range of play and enriching activities before, during and after the school day. Extended schools – which all schools will become – offer access to a range of out of school opportunities. We will promote further investment in outdoor play facilities on school sites through our school capital programmes, such as Building Schools for the Future.

1.48 Local authorities and communities have lead a role in promoting play. DCSF will work with the Department for Culture, Media and Sport and Communities and Local Government (CLG) to look for ways to support councils and the third sector to work with local communities to provide better physical environments, focusing in the first instance on disadvantaged communities, and ensuring new spaces to play are accessible to disabled children.

> *"Local communities are losing their togetherness, more people are working, we have to meet demands for bills, but this means kids being pushed here and there and losing the caring part of communities. Stop shutting clubs, parks, etc, more people need to care to run voluntary projects, especially for kids who are disadvantaged in a big way." (Parent/work with children and young people, Online survey)*

1.49 The Tellus2 survey, which children in schools fill out, contains for the first time a question on children's satisfaction with parks and green spaces, which local authorities can use to assess satisfaction levels and track progress over time.

1.50 **To create more safe places to play, the Government will invest £225 million over the next three years.** This will offer every local authority capital funding that would allow up to 3,500 playgrounds to be rebuilt or renewed and made accessible to children with disabilities. And because we have identified particular problems for children aged 8–13 finding places to play we will support up to 30 new pilots of supervised play parks aimed at 8–13-year-olds in disadvantaged areas. We will support 30 play pathfinders which will test innovative approaches to promoting and supporting play spaces. We will also pilot new volunteering schemes that will support play.

1.51 This investment builds on the support for play sites already provided by BIG lottery funding and the associated local play strategies that local authorities have created. To back up the new investment being made we will publish a new national strategy on play in the first half of 2008.

> ## Case study – Play parks in Finland
>
> Helsinki has 71 play parks in different parts of the city, which the city council view as strong and long-standing amenities. Parks bring together free play and positive activities in safe, supervised settings, and are fully accessible to disabled children. The parks are at residents' disposal all year round, operate on an open-access basis and are usually free of charge, including a free meal for children. For example Vallila play park acts as a meeting point for families with children, as well as other residents. The aim of the park is to give a safe place for children to play in the afternoons, to promote community cohesion and to support parenthood. The outdoor areas provide activities during all seasons, while the indoor areas have a kitchenette and designated areas for supervised indoor activities. Regular organised activities include outdoor play and games, singing, arts and crafts. Special activities include trips to children's theatres.

1.52 Drawing on lessons from these Pathfinders and evaluations of existing approaches, we will extend capital funding to every local authority in England not already covered by the Play Pathfinders to support the delivery of stimulating local places to play. We would like to see strong participation of children, families and communities in the design of new spaces. This is part of the community empowerment agenda and will be critical to ensuring spaces meet local needs and wants. The play strategy will support individuals in communities to take a professional role by **providing funding to enable 4,000 play workers to achieve recognised play qualifications, and within that to enable a core of professionally qualified new graduate leaders to emerge.**

1.53 We will work with CLG on reviews of statutory planning guidance, and in partnership with registered social landlords to improve the quality of play environments in some of the most deprived areas. Again DCSF will work with CLG to produce guidance for planners on good play space. CLG will highlight to chief planning officers the importance of outdoor play for children. We will improve training for planners, highways officers and green space managers and work with local authorities and others to make child-friendly public space a feature of eco-towns and major new housing developments in the Growth Areas, Growth Points, and the legacy for the Olympic Park.

Box 1.3: Greater London Authority (GLA) play and informal recreation policy

The GLA have recognised how critical it is for local authorities to join-up their policy for children with that on planning, transport and the environment, and recognise the important contribution that child-friendly places can make to sustainable community strategies. Their *Further Alterations To The London Plan*, due to be published in early 2008, contains a new policy requiring all housing developments in London to provide 10 sq m of high quality, accessible play and informal recreation space for every child to be housed. The policy and the supplementary guide have gathered weight through consultation and are being used successfully in determining whether the Mayor directs refusal of housing applications referred to him. All housing applications are expected to show how play and recreation needs have been met and how the proposals relate to the borough play strategy.

Positive structured activities

1.54 Participation in positive, structured activities such as drama, music, team sports, or volunteering boosts a child's resilience and can reduce mental health problems and problem behaviour.

1.55 The Government has recently committed £265 million **to provide disadvantaged children and young people with access to positive extended school activities of their choosing**. We will look at how the new Play Pathfinders can support this.

Improving children's health

1.56 Good health is vital if children and young people are to enjoy their childhood and achieve their full potential. Healthy habits established early provide the basis for lifelong health and wellbeing.

1.57 The Government ten-year vision for children's and young people's health, building on the National Service Framework for Children, Young People and Maternity services is that:

- infant mortality continues to fall, and inequalities between poor and advantaged families are substantially reduced – supporting the Government's target to reduce health inequalities by 10 per cent by 2010 as measured by infant mortality and life expectancy;

- young children thrive in the first years of life, with more tailored support for parents and parenting and better early support for individual needs;

- all schools help children learn to value their health and wellbeing, eat well and keep fit and active in a healthy school environment;

- overweight and obesity among children and young people falls back by 2020 to 2000 prevalence levels;

- young people show lower levels of risky adolescent health behaviour, evidenced in reduced drinking and sustained reduction in under-18 conception rates and sexually transmitted diseases (addressed in Chapter 6);

- children's emotional wellbeing improves, supported by better Child and Adolescent Mental Health Services; and

- disabled children and their families see a step change in their experience of services and in the outcomes for disabled children.

1.58 The next steps will be set out in a new Children and Young People's Health Strategy being developed with the Department of Health (DH) and is due to be published in spring 2008. It will build on the National Service Framework for Children, Young People and Maternity services and be taken forward in the context of the NHS Next Steps Review, *Our NHS, Our Future*, led by Lord Darzi which reports in 2008.

1.59 Achieving our vision will require all services for children to work together. The Government's key principles for this partnership are:

- supporting children and families to meet their own health goals, as families are the key influences on children's health;

- the NHS prioritising children and young people as an investment in the future health of the nation while other children's services acknowledge and play their role in improving child health. The 2008–09 NHS Operating Framework will make clear the priority the Government attaches to children and young people's health; and

- strong local partnerships including joint needs assessments and commissioning between local authorities and Primary Care Trusts.

Pregnancy, infancy and the first years of life

1.60 New research into brain development, attachment and the impact of stress in pregnancy confirms our view that pregnancy and the first years of life are the most important formative stage. Good health in this stage and services that work with parents, are critically important. DCSF and DH will work together to secure improvements in health, wellbeing and child development in pregnancy, infancy and the first years of life.

1.61 DH, with DCSF and CLG, will shortly be putting in place an action plan to reduce and tackle inequalities in infant mortality. An updated Child Health Promotion Programme will improve access to ante-natal services and more tailored and accessible support for parents.

1.62 In children's early years, health services are often the service parents use most. Locating General Practice (GP) surgeries near focal points of the community (for example shopping centres or schools) means that families can more easily find the services they want, and that children are more likely to get the health support they need when they need it.

1.63 Alongside GPs, Sure Start Children's Centres are providing fully integrated services to local children and their families, with multi-agency teams made up of midwives, nursery nurses and a range of early years and family support staff. This will be particularly important for children who require early intervention, for example for reasons of delayed development. The early years are an important time to establish good habits of eating and active play. We are supporting all Sure Start Children's Centres to promote of healthy lifestyles, and to provide advice and support for parents on diet and nutrition and physical activity.

Box 1.4: Health visiting services and the Child Health Promotion Programme

Across GP and Children's Centres, health visitors play a vital role in maximising the reach of services and helping excluded families to access community-based support.

The current review of the Child Health Promotion Programme will consider how the NHS can best lead the delivery of a high-quality, evidence-based, visible and popular health promotion programme that is universal but tailored to the needs of children and families – both fathers and mothers – at individual, community and population levels. The most at risk children and families need an intensive, preventative programme that begins early enough to make a difference. The revised programme will include evidence-based programmes for families with greater risks, including the Nurse Family Partnership Programme, which is beginning to show early evidence of improved outcomes for families.

The role of schools

1.64 Schools play a vital role in promoting physical and mental health, and emotional wellbeing, underpinned now by a duty to promote the wellbeing of pupils in the Education and Inspections Act 2006, guidance on which will be issued early in 2008.

1.65 This role is being strengthened through:

- ensuring that every school is offering a wide range of extended activities and services from 8am to 6pm;

- the Healthy Schools Programme, with all schools expected to be working towards Healthy School Status by 2009, and at least 75 per cent having achieved accreditation;

- our school building programmes, including Building Schools for the Future, with better school kitchens and dining rooms; and better PE, sport, play and outdoor recreation facilities, and facilities designed with the delivery of mainstream services in mind;

- efforts to ensure local authorities work with schools and parents to increase cycling and walking to and from school; and

- better techniques for early identification and assessment of additional need, and more effective joined-up working to support swift and easy referral to specialist services.

1.66 By 2011 we will have invested £650 million to improve the quality of school food. Working with the School Food Trust, we have set demanding minimum standards for the provision of food across the school day and improved the quality and availability of training for school cooks and caterers, which will continue with the creation of a network of regional training centres from 2008. We are providing school kitchens in areas of greatest need; and from September 2008 all secondary school pupils will have an entitlement to learn to cook. While we have seen a decline in take-up of school lunches, we are confident we can reverse this by working to persuade children, young people and parents of the benefits of good quality school food.

Child obesity

1.67 Obesity is one of the most serious challenges for children from all backgrounds and is linked to a number of poor outcomes, including type 2 diabetes, adverse social and psychological consequences, cardio-vascular disease, some cancers, and osteoarthritis. It is a growing problem in England – in 2005 nearly one in five children between the ages of 2 and 15, both boys and girls, were obese compared to around one in eight in 1997. The biggest risk factor is family lifestyle: in families where both parents are overweight or obese, children are six times more likely to be so too, compared to children whose parents are of a healthy weight. In addition, there are some smaller differences associated with ethnicity, socio-economic status, education level and inner-city living.

1.68 We are working across government to tackle child obesity, to meet **our goal to reduce the proportion of overweight and obese children in the population to 2000 levels by 2020.** A national strategy and action plan to be published in early 2008 will set out plans for tackling obesity in children and adults. To complement national action, the NHS National Operating Framework for 2008–09 has established tackling obesity as one of the national requirements for Primary Care Trusts (PCTs). All PCTs will be required to work closely with local authorities and their partners (within a joint strategic planning and commissioning framework) to develop a local strategy setting out how they will effectively tackle the challenge of rising obesity levels in their areas, with a particular focus on interventions aimed at children and families.

1.69 The section above on active childhood sets out further action to take to develop active play and healthy environments for children to encourage children and young people to be physically active.

Emotional health and mental wellbeing

1.70 Emotional wellbeing and good mental health are crucial for every aspect of a child's life, now and in the future. These capabilities are derived from a loving and supportive family and a breadth of positive experiences in childhood. Strong social and emotional skills are essential to success in life and work, but the evidence shows that children from disadvantaged backgrounds tend to possess them to a lesser extent than their more advantaged peers. We want to ensure all children and young people develop these skills.

Promoting social and emotional skills

1.71 Good social and emotional skills are vital for healthy personal development. They build resilience and reduce the likelihood of engaging in risky behaviour, and support educational achievement, employment and earnings, and relationships in adulthood.

1.72 We want all children develop strong social and emotional skills from the early years on. The Government is working to promote attachment and bonding in the first years of life, including through extending maternity and paternity leave. The Early Years Foundation Stage, which will be fully operational from September 2008, looks at the whole range of a child's cognitive and non-cognitive development. The Social and Emotional Aspects of Learning programme, which we expect the great majority of schools to be implementing by 2011, provides a whole school approach to promoting these skills. We have announced investment of £60 million in piloting school-based emotional wellbeing and mental health services. Chapter 3 sets out our plans to bring these frameworks together in a more coherent way, and ensure schools are effectively encouraged to give social and emotional skills priority as part of wider work on personal and social development.

1.73 Because social and emotional skills are of such importance to unlocking children's potential, we will develop a national measure of children and young people's social and emotional skills at key transition points in their education, **and one of our 2020 goals will be to enhance children and young people's wellbeing, particularly at key transition points**.

Child and Adolescent Mental Health Services

1.74 Effective and responsive mental health services are vital to support children and young people with emerging or existing conditions. We have increased investment in Children and Adolescent Mental Health Services (CAMHS), increasing capacity, reducing waiting times, and increasing the numbers of children and young people benefiting from specialist CAMHS. We will also increase the number of specialist CAMHS beds for those with greatest need, and will eliminate the inappropriate use of adult psychiatric wards for under 16-year-olds by November 2008.

1.75 However, challenges remain. Specialist services are not meeting the needs of some of our most vulnerable children, with complex and challenging needs. In 2005 only 23 per cent of local authorities reported that they had fully operational partnership working to meet the needs of this group. The effectiveness of planning, commissioning and management arrangements have been highlighted as an issue.

1.76 **We will commission an externally-led review of CAMHS** with a remit to:

- take stock of progress to date and to identify how mainstream and universal services could play a more effective role in promoting the emotional wellbeing and mental health of children, young people and their families – including looking at the training of staff;

- identify practical solutions to current barriers in the delivery of integrated care pathways at a service delivery and strategic level;

- advise on key gaps in the delivery strategy to support the CAMHS elements of the Child Health and Wellbeing PSA;

- develop priority actions for national, regional and local stakeholders in delivering the proposed vision of emotional health and wellbeing; and

- clarify the performance management arrangements necessary to support delivery including the development of robust local and national outcome indicators.

Child poverty

1.77 The Government is committed to halving child poverty by 2010 and eradicating it by 2020. The number of children in relative poverty fell by 600,000 between 1998 and 2006. However, poverty still blights the childhood of a significant minority of children in England, and harms their prospects for adult life – and the prospects for their children. Particular groups, such as disabled children and those from black and minority ethnic groups are especially likely to live in poverty.

1.78 The *Time to Talk* consultation showed that children and young people were particularly concerned by issues of inequality, and by how hard it is to live on a low income.

1.79 If we are to eradicate child poverty we need to break the cycle of poverty that passes from generation to generation by:

- tackling the causes of inequalities directly by reducing poverty among children today by lifting family incomes, supporting work and improving the conditions for family life; and

- improving the prospects for the most disadvantaged children by closing gaps in educational, health and other outcomes, thereby making it less likely that their children will live in poverty.

1.80 For children today, parental employment provides the best sustainable route out of poverty. Families are better off in work than on benefits, both financially and in terms of health and wellbeing. And because the attitudes and expectations parents have directly shape the aspirations of their children, the benefits of being in work pass on to the next generation.

1.81 But services must also be at the heart of tackling inter-generational poverty. The Government will ensure that all children have access to a world-class education which supports their cognitive, social and emotional skill development so that no child is left to fall behind. We will support families to help their children reach their full potential. We must also ensure that children growing up in families on low incomes are able to live in safe, cohesive communities, just like other children, to give them the best start in life.

Box 1.5: Tackling child poverty

Policies set out across this Plan will strengthen our approach to both tackling child poverty in the short term and helping to eradicate it over the next decade, through supporting families, communities and children of all ages:

- more tailored and accessible support for parents and increased investment in high quality outreach services;

- extending the free entitlement to 15 hours per week of early learning and childcare for all 3- and 4-year-olds as well as 2-year-olds in disadvantaged areas and investing to improve the quality of early years provision;

- making childcare available for children up to the age of 14 and providing more accessible childcare for families with disabled children;

- building a network of Sure Start Children's Centres, delivering better training and employment support for parents and expanding the Family Literacy, Language and Numeracy programme;

- an intensified focus on ensuring all children and young people leave school with the skills they need to thrive through investment in workforce development, one-to-one help for those at risk of falling behind, a new 14–19 curriculum and a greater focus on personal, social and emotional skills throughout the system;

- a priority on early identification and intervention to resolve issues that may be holding children back from achieving their potential. Investment in tackling health inequalities, providing things to do and places to go for children and young people and support for emotional, behavioural and mental health problems; and

- ensuring separated parents and their children get to keep more of the maintenance paid to them. By the end of 2008 parents with care claiming the main income-related benefits will be able to keep the first £20 per week of any maintenance paid before their benefit is affected. This doubles to £40 per week from April 2010. This will benefit some 350,000 children and will lift around 50,000 children out of poverty.

1.82 Ending child poverty requires a sustained national, local and regional effort across all agencies, service providers and professionals, but also businesses and communities. Regional and local economic and regeneration strategies need to address the needs of the most disadvantaged families. The new Child Poverty Unit which is a joint unit of the Department for Children, Schools and Families and the Department for Work and Pensions will play a lead co-ordinating role, as the Government pursues its multi-faceted child poverty strategy which includes transport, health and regeneration as well as employment, skills and the tax and benefit system on the way towards making our ambitious but vital goal of eradicating child poverty by 2020 a reality.

Box 1.6: Housing

Housing affects life chances. Cold, damp housing harms children's health and can contribute to post-natal depression. The development of babies and young children in poor housing conditions can be significantly affected. Children growing up in such conditions are 25 per cent more likely to suffer severe ill-health and disability during childhood or early adulthood. One in ten children live in overcrowded accommodation. This can have an adverse effect on child wellbeing, leaving them with no place to do their homework or play with friends and more likely to underachieve at school. Teenagers are more likely to stay out on the streets, and many parents experience stress. In the worst cases, overcrowding is associated with domestic violence and relationship breakdown. Children in homeless families often experience significant disruption to their education. Those placed in temporary accommodation outside their local area can face travelling long distances to stay at their schools or the disruption of a new start at a new school. To tackle these issues, we will now take the following further action:

1. Since 1997 we have already reduced the number of children in bad housing (non-decent or overcrowded homes and temporary accommodation) by over 1.4 million. By 2010 we will increase this figure to over 2 million.

2. A further £11 billion will be invested in further improvements to the quality of social housing over the next three years, and £1.1 billion in private sector renewal, including tackling cold, damp family homes and putting in modern central heating.

3. As set out in the 2007 Green Paper *Homes for the future: more affordable, more sustainable*, the Government will invest in more social housing and support more homes to be provided overall, including more family homes. As stated in our Public Service Agreement on increasing long-term housing supply and affordability (PSA 20), our ambition is to build an additional 3 million homes by 2020, along with the necessary supporting infrastructure to support this housing growth such as schools.

4. Communities and Local Government will shortly publish an action plan to tackle overcrowding. We are committed to updating the statutory overcrowding standards to the bedroom standard, which sets the notional number of bedrooms for a household, and will use the action plan and work in a series of pathfinders to establish the cost and a suitable timeframe for doing this.

5. The Homelessness Code of Guidance for local authorities states that housing authorities should, wherever possible, secure accommodation that is as close as possible to where families were previously living so that they can retain established links with key services. In spring 2008, jointly with Communities and Local Government, we will publish good practice guidance and protocols on better working between housing and children's services at local level to meet the needs of children and young people.

Conclusion and next steps

1.83 This chapter has set out our priority actions in relation to health and wellbeing against a number of key areas: supporting families with the challenges of today, promoting active and healthy childhood – including physical, emotional and mental health, and tackling child poverty. The next steps will be to work with partners to deliver these changes through the new strategies on children and young people's health, play and reviews of Child and Adolescent Mental Health Services, and further work on areas such as family breakdown. There will be an implementation plan to take forward policies announced in *Care Matters*.

1.84 Safeguarding children is also critical to ensuring their health and wellbeing; the next chapter sets out our approach to ensuring all children are safe.

Chapter 2: Safe and sound

Safeguard the young and vulnerable

Executive summary

2.1 Keeping children and young people safe from harm must be the priority and responsibility of us all. However, children need also to be able to learn, have new experiences and enjoy their childhoods, so we will help families strike the right balance between keeping children safe and allowing them the freedom they need. So we will:

- publish Dr Tanya Byron's review on the potential risks to children from exposure to harmful or inappropriate content on the internet and in video games;

- commission an independent assessment of the impact of the commercial world on children's wellbeing;

- fund a new home safety equipment scheme to prevent the accidents which happen to young children in the home;

- encourage local authorities to create 20mph zones where appropriate because they can reduce child pedestrian deaths by 70 per cent; and

- strengthen the complaints procedure for parents whose children experience bullying.

2.2 Government also has a responsibility to put in place the right frameworks and systems for safeguarding children and young people, working in partnership with key national and local organisations and so we will:

- publish the *Staying Safe Action Plan* in early 2008, responding to the *Staying Safe* consultation; and

- ensure that schools and local authorities take a proportionate approach to health and safety to allow children to take risks while staying safe.

Vision for the next decade

2.3 The Government is determined to maintain a relentless focus on the safety of children and young people and the vulnerable. Our vision for the next decade is to make a reality of our aspiration to make children's safety everyone's responsibility. We want a society where everyone understands the issues and what they can do, and where everyone works together to help children and young people stay safe.

2.4 Through the publication of the new Public Service Agreement (PSA) to improve children's and young people's safety we have shown our determination to deliver tangible improvements and to be held accountable for doing so. The PSA is underpinned by four key indicators:

- percentage of children who have experienced bullying;

- percentage of children referred to children's social care who received an initial assessment within seven working days;

- hospital admissions caused by unintentional and deliberate injuries to children and young people; and

- preventable child deaths as recorded through child death review panel processes.

2.5 In many ways, children and young people today are safer than in previous generations and have opportunities that their parents and grandparents would not have dreamed of, for instance access to new technologies, travel and leisure, and improvements in educational standards. Rates of sudden infant deaths have fallen, and rates of accidents are down, including on the roads.

2.6 But, as the three Expert Groups recognised, society today is more complex than in previous generations. Children and young people have more choice, but also face new challenges. Family structures are changing, communities are more diverse, and some of the traditional support networks, particularly for parents, are not available to many families. Growth in new technologies has brought wonderful new opportunities for education, information, communication and leisure but it has also brought new opportunities for people who wish to exploit and harm children. And some groups of children and young people, such as children living in deprived areas, children in care, disabled children, migrant children and unaccompanied asylum-seeking children, are more vulnerable to harm than others.

2.7 Since summer 2007, we have engaged many stakeholders, including parents and young people, in a consultation about how to improve children's safety, *Staying Safe*, set out in Box 2.1. The concerns that were raised correspond with those that we heard in the *Time to Talk* consultation:

- parents raised particular concerns about road safety (35 per cent), followed by bullying (26 per cent) and drugs and alcohol (20 per cent);

- many adults responding to the consultation (57 per cent) said that, as a society, we are not good at striking the right balance between keeping children safe and allowing them opportunities to experience and manage risk; and

- children and young people spoke more about specific safety concerns. In particular they were worried about having safe places to go, safe transport at night, and being allowed to 'hang out' in groups – where they felt safer.

  "safe places to hang around and meet mates. Somewhere that's well lit and maybe CCTV." (*Young person's response to* Staying Safe)

2.8 We are not starting from scratch. Over the past few years, we have introduced new legislation, policies and structures designed to make children safer. Safeguarding is recognised by more people and organisations as an important part of their work than ever before. It remains a strong public concern and it is a priority for the Government and the Inspectorates in our work to challenge and support local services.

2.9 The Government will publish the *Staying Safe Action Plan* in early 2008, responding to the *Staying Safe* consultation and setting out in more detail an extensive programme of action to improve all children's and young people's safety. This will include areas suggested by consultation responses as needing further action, such as the safeguarding of disabled children, the sexual exploitation of children, the safety of young people in the youth justice system, and safety on the streets. In addition, the forthcoming Youth Crime Action Plan, discussed in more detail in Chapter 6, will address issues including victimisation and serious youth violence.

Key areas for reform

2.10 A comprehensive programme to improve children's safety will be set out in the *Staying Safe Action Plan*. This chapter considers some of the key areas for reform and sets out how we will build on progress already made to:

- promote understanding and management of risks;
- reduce risks associated with media and the commercial world;
- reduce accidents, both on the roads and in the home, particularly within vulnerable families;
- tackle bullying;
- ensure that children's and young people's concerns are listened to;
- foster greater collaboration to keep children safe, through effective Local Safeguarding Children Boards; and
- prevent unsuitable people from working with children.

Box 2.1: *Staying Safe* consultation

In July 2007, we published *Staying Safe*, a consultation on a cross-government strategy on children's safety. We also published a young people's version of *Staying Safe* and held discussion groups with children and young people to ensure that we reflected their concerns and ideas about what will make them feel safer. Between July and October, there were over a thousand written responses to the consultation from children and young people, parents, members of the general public and people working with children.

We wanted to raise awareness and understanding of all aspects of children's and young people's safety. *Staying Safe* set out what is happening both nationally and locally to keep children safe and looked at areas where the Government and its partners could be doing more to improve children's safety, as well as how we can all make action already underway or planned more coherent and more effective.

The consultation identified 11 areas for new or additional action, and made proposals to plug gaps in the framework or address specific issues.

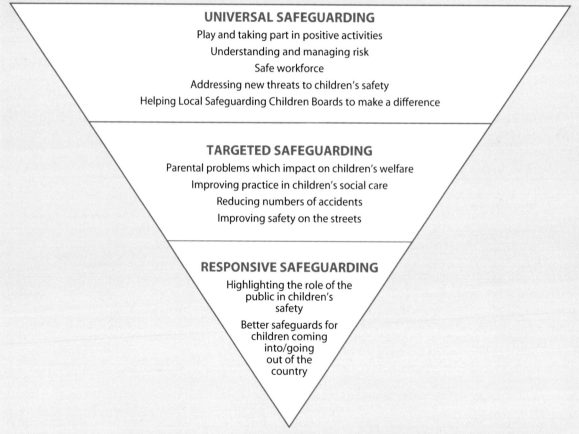

As set out above, the Government will publish the *Staying Safe Action Plan* in early 2008. This will respond to the Staying Safe consultation, and set out further action to improve children's and young people's safety, and will be underpinned by the new Public Service Agreement.

Promoting understanding and management of risks

2.11 Bringing up children is the responsibility of families and carers. Government has a role to play in helping parents and carers to strike the right balance between protecting their children and managing risk and allowing them to learn and explore new situations safely.

2.12 The *Staying Safe* consultation document underlined the importance of everyone understanding children's safety issues and being prepared to play a role in keeping children safe. It made several proposals to improve awareness and understanding through communications, including to parents about risks their children are likely to face, and to the public to encourage them to play an active role in protecting children and young people from harm.

2.13 Responses to the consultation were generally in favour of giving parents more information about safety and encouraging the public to be more involved in keeping children safe. We will promote better understanding of management of risks to children's safety by launching a new communications campaign to provide parents with information about risk and harm faced by children, with a focus on high-risk households, and to encourage the general public to play a role in keeping children safe. We will announce further details in the *Staying Safe Action Plan*.

2.14 **We will ensure that schools and local authorities take a proportionate approach to health and safety to allow children to take risks while staying safe.** We are particularly interested in addressing situations where perceptions of the requirements of health and safety rules, or local interpretation of those rules, can be such that they prevent pupils from enjoying valuable learning experiences both within school and on school visits. In addition, we will continue to expect schools to cover understanding and management of risk as part of safety education and during learning outside the classroom, where we advise schools to involve pupils in undertaking risk assessments.

Reducing risks associated with media and the commercial world

2.15 New technologies are bringing major changes to the way young people communicate, learn about the world, and keep in touch with their friends and families. These changes are overwhelmingly positive, providing children today with opportunities to learn, communicate and have fun unthought of in previous generations. The Government wants to help parents and their children get the best from these new technologies, so that children grow up prepared for a world in which using technology, like the internet, is as commonplace as writing with a pen and paper.

Risks from potentially harmful media content

2.16 The Government will continue to help children and parents get the most out of the opportunities of today's media and communications technology. We will continue to work to ensure all children have access to the internet, in particular through our Home Access Initiative, which is considering ways to ensure that all children can access technology whenever and wherever it is appropriate for their learning (see also Chapter 3). And we recognise the importance of ensuring that everyone in Britain has the confidence and knowledge to make the most of today's varied media. Therefore the Government will continue to work together with industry and educators to improve the media literacy of all children and parents.

2.17 While we recognise the many benefits new technologies can bring, we know that we need to protect children and young people from inappropriate or potentially harmful material. Children who use digital technologies have access to a huge range of information, but there may be some content that parents do not want their children to see. That is why in September 2007 the Government asked Dr Tanya Byron to examine the risks to children and young people from exposure to potentially harmful or inappropriate material on the internet and in video games using her expertise in child development and working with parents, carers and families.

2.18 Over the first three months, the review has already generated an important debate, with engagement from a very wide range of industry stakeholders, parents, children and young people. Two calls for evidence have been issued, including one aimed specifically at children and young people. Children and young people often know more about the latest developments in new technology and video games than adults do, so hearing what they have to say about the benefits and risks will be a critical complement to the academic research in this field.

2.19 Parents will have different views on what they want their children to experience at different ages and stages of development. So a key theme for the review will be to consider ways of ensuring that parents have the information and the confidence they need to make informed decisions about how their children use new technologies. They need to be empowered to choose from current and future tools that can help them manage the risks of potentially inappropriate content on the internet and in video games.

2.20 Dr Byron is assessing existing mechanisms for protecting the safety and welfare of children and young people online and when playing video games. This includes a wide ranging and in depth analysis of the current regulatory frameworks in these areas, and the review will set out ways of securing the action needed from industry and government to protect children. The review is seeking to develop recommendations based on a shared approach between industry, government and society.

2.21 Dr Byron will report back to the Government in March 2008 on the evidence about the benefits and potential risks, what is already happening to address them and what more can be done, to empower parents and protect children.

Commercial activity

2.22 In addition to their increasing use of technology, children today are also more involved in commercial activity than previous generations. The last decade in particular has seen children become ever more involved in the commercial world, along with an increase in the range of commercial activities aimed at children. Evidence suggests that recent years have seen the size of markets for children's products and services increase, and young people's commercial awareness rise. At the same time the amount of money children are spending has risen, while the age at which they begin shopping has fallen.

2.23 This is often a positive change. The market now provides increased choice and is more responsive to children's preferences. Beginning to understand the commercial world is part of growing up, and also an important part of preparing for a future role as a demanding consumer in adulthood.

2.24 However, some evidence suggests that the combination of a lowering in the age at which children begin to engage with the commercial world, along with an increase in the quantity of commercial messages targeted at children, may have some outcomes which are detrimental for children's wellbeing. Overall, however, this is an area where evidence is not clear. In particular, there is a gap in understanding properly the impact that cumulative exposure to shopping, advertising and commercial messaging may have on children's wellbeing, particularly at a young age.

2.25 The Government is also considering a range of other policies related to children's media and commercial engagement, in areas where there is already a growing body of evidence. Therefore, **the Government will commission an independent assessment of the overall impact of the commercial world on children's wellbeing**. We will ask the assessors to look into the changing nature and extent of children's commercial engagement, the impact on their wellbeing and the views of parents and children. In particular, the assessment will investigate particular areas where exposure to commercialism might be causing harm to children. We hope that this increased evidence base will lead to a stronger consensus about what is acceptable practice for a socially responsible commercial community.

2.26 The Government is working with public service broadcasters and the regulator Ofcom to consider a range of issues that have relevance to children's media and commercial engagement. In particular, Ofcom is currently undertaking a review of Public Service Television Broadcasting, which will examine the future of children's broadcasting in the UK. The Department for Children, Schools and Families (DCSF) welcomes Ofcom's recently published research on the *Future of Children's Television Programming* that informs the current review. We also agree with its conclusion that the future provision of new UK-originated content for children, especially in important areas like drama and factual programmes that are aimed at older children, looks uncertain other than from the BBC. The Government recognises the importance of high quality programming to the lives of children and parents. The DCSF will engage fully with Ofcom's review to ensure that the views of children, young people and families are considered, and work to secure the future of quality children's television in Britain.

Reducing the number of accidents

2.27 Accidents are the biggest cause of non-medical deaths for children, particularly on the roads. But most accidents occur in the home, and disadvantaged families are particularly vulnerable.

Safer roads

2.28 The Government's road safety policies have been effective over the long term. In 2006 the number of children aged up to 15 years who were seriously injured or killed in road accidents in Great Britain was 52 per cent below the 1994–98 average, which is the baseline for the Government's 2010 casualty reduction targets. However, the number of children killed in 2006 was higher than the record low in 2005 and overall we have made less progress for older children than for younger children. So we still need to make improvements to children's safety and reduce the numbers killed and injured on the roads.

2.29 Road safety education in schools can play an important part in improving road safety for children, including practical roadside training. So we need to learn from the best examples and encourage more schools to deliver good quality road safety education, especially for older children. Parents and carers also help to teach their children about road safety and have a continuing influence every time they travel with their children – including older children. We should do all we can to improve the support they need to do this and encourage them to provide a good example to their children.

2.30 Car and other vehicle drivers also have a responsibility for child road safety. All measures to improve road safety more generally will help to improve the safety and wellbeing of children. This includes improvements to driver training and testing, publicity to encourage better driving behaviour in areas such as speed, drink-driving and mobile phone use, and police enforcement to encourage compliance with legislation in these areas.

2.31 Local authorities can support child-friendly public space through speed limit reduction and traffic calming in residential areas and places where children play. Research has shown that child pedestrian accidents were reduced by 70 per cent after the introduction of 20 mph zones in the UK. 20 mph zones are particularly appropriate where there is an existing record of accidents to children occurring over an area, or where concentrations of pedestrians and/or cyclists exist or are anticipated. They can help protect children walking and cycling to and from play sites and school, and may help to encourage other children to walk or cycle. **We encourage local authorities to create 20 mph zones where appropriate because they can reduce child pedestrian deaths by 70 per cent**.

2.32 While 20 mph zones greatly reduce the risk of death and serious injury, it is not eliminated. To make streets themselves spaces for play, further action is often needed. In the right places, Home Zones have the potential to transform the quality of life in our local communities by restoring the balance between traffic and people living in a street. Home Zones are residential areas where the streets are designed to limit vehicles to very low speeds. The aim is to improve the quality of life by making them places for people (including children playing) instead of simply corridors for motor traffic. They can bring communities together, making streets more sociable and better places to live. We encourage councils to support applications for Home Zones.

2.33 The Department for Transport will be contacting Local Highway Authorities to highlight the need to have regard to children's wellbeing and safety when implementing transport policy.

Reducing accidents in the home

2.34 Although the most serious accidents happen on the roads, the majority of children's accidents take place in the home. This is particularly an issue for younger children. Children under the age of 5 carry a disproportionate burden of injuries from falls and fires. They suffer nearly 45 per cent of all severe burns and scalds. About half of these happen in the kitchen, and approximately 50 per cent of all injuries to children under 5 occur in the home. In 1997 and 1998, children under 5 represented 71 per cent of childhood fatalities from fire. Within the PSA to improve children's and young people's safety, we have included an indicator on hospital admissions caused by accidental and deliberate injuries, and government departments will work together with the aim of reducing accidental injuries and deaths to children.

2.35 There are many excellent schemes around the country which help children and young people to understand risks to their safety and how these can be managed (see the case study below). There are also many teaching materials available for schools, particularly for the personal, social and health education curriculum. These materials aim to help children and young people to keep themselves safe in a range of situations, including at home, at school and while playing. **As part of the *Staying Safe Action Plan*, we will consider ways in which these types of learning could be extended so that more children and young people can benefit**.

Case study: Learning About Safety by Experiencing Risk (LASER)

The Royal Society for the Prevention of Accidents (RoSPA) LASER project was funded for three years from 1999 by the Department of Health to produce good practice guidelines for interactive safety education schemes, such as the Crucial Crew and Junior Citizens. The initiatives focus their efforts on accident prevention and safety promotion, particularly for children aged 9–11 years old. Emphasis is very much on the belief that children learn by doing, and the scenarios are made as interactive as possible. The children learn by experiencing risky situations for example an unsafe kitchen, a smoke-filled bedroom or the scene of a road traffic accident. The scenarios typically last for ten minutes. The children are split into small groups of about six and move round the different scenarios.

The LASER schemes are set up throughout the UK and most involve the collaboration of the emergency services, local authorities and other local partners. The majority are temporary schemes set up for a limited period each year, but there are also nine permanent centres around the country. The Department of Health is currently funding RoSPA to develop an accreditation process for safety centres, as a voluntary quality assurance programme, so that safety centres can demonstrate their credibility and educational value.

2.36 The *Staying Safe* consultation document highlighted the risks faced by children in lower socio-economic groups, particularly in the home. Children of parents who have never worked or who are long-term unemployed are 13 times more likely to die from unintentional injury and 37 times more likely to die as a result of exposure to smoke, fire and flames than children of parents in higher managerial and professional occupations.

"Maybe there should be more available, more money, for things like the child gates and someone to put them in for you." (Parent)

2.37 Many families cannot afford basic safety equipment, such as stair gates, fireguards, socket covers, which can prevent accidents from occurring in the home. While some local areas have schemes which provide low cost or free home safety equipment to families, these schemes are not universally available. In light of the consultation responses to *Staying Safe* and to reduce the numbers of accidents amongst younger children, **we have recently announced that we will fund a new home safety equipment scheme targeted at families in disadvantaged areas, totalling £18 million over three years**.

Tackling bullying

2.38 About a third of all pupils experience bullying. Bullying can destroy lives and have immeasurable impact on young people's confidence, self-esteem, mental health and social and emotional development. Research has shown that bullying can have long-term negative effects, including a loss of confidence and mental health problems and can affect job prospects.

2.39 Bullying of any kind is unacceptable. Some groups of children and young people are particularly vulnerable to bullying. The Department for Education and Skills published guidance for schools on tackling bullying around race, religion and culture in March 2006 and followed this up with guidance on how to prevent and tackle homophobic bullying earlier this year. We have asked the National Strategies and the Anti-Bullying Alliance to work with local authorities and schools to ensure the guidance is effectively implemented on the ground and will monitor the situation closely. We will produce **guidance to help schools tackle the bullying of children with special educational needs (SEN) and disabilities** and will publish this in spring 2008.

2.40 Although much progress has been made to address bullying, more needs to be done. We are embedding effective anti-bullying practice in schools, via the recently launched arrangements through National Strategies for targeting schools that have particular bullying issues, and we have announced a two-year pilot on effective peer mentoring practice to promote positive peer relationships. We published comprehensive guidance to help schools prevent and tackle cyberbullying as part of our *Safe to Learn* suite of guidance and have also run an information campaign for children and young people called *Laugh at it, and you're part of it*. The new Cyberbullying Taskforce made up of internet providers, mobile phone companies, children's charities and teachers' unions will take forward a programme of work to tackle cyberbullying, and we will work with them to monitor the situation closely and consider whether any additional measures need to be introduced to tackle this problem.

2.41 **We will also look to strengthen the way that bullying complaints are dealt with in the light of the Children's Commissioner's report, and will consider how to address bullying outside schools in the *Staying Safe Action Plan*.**

Listening to children's and young people's concerns

2.42 If children and young people are being harmed or fear they are at risk, it is important they have somewhere to turn to and someone who will listen and help. We have already committed to investing **£30 million in ChildLine and other NSPCC helpline services over the next four years**.

2.43 This new funding will allow the NSPCC to expand ChildLine and its other helpline services significantly and improve them so that more children can be given the advice and help that can be so important. This will include expanding what is currently the NSPCC's 'there4me' service which offers live one-to-one counselling with an online adviser.

2.44 There are particular risks to disabled children with severe communications difficulties and we need to ensure that they can raise concerns about harm, especially where they are in care. As announced in *Care Matters*, we will require independent reviewing officers to have the skills in communicating with disabled children in care, or to commission a specialist who has these skills, to ensure the views of children are put forward effectively.

Collaborating to keep children safe

2.45 The Children Act 2004 introduced a new duty to make arrangements to safeguard and promote the welfare of children, which falls on a range of organisations including local authorities, health services, police forces and youth offending teams. This followed a similar duty on schools in the Education Act 2002. The revised *Working Together to Safeguard Children* (2006) provides a comprehensive framework of guidance on how local agencies should collaborate to keep children and young people safe.

2.46 Statutory Local Safeguarding Children Boards (LSCBs) were established in every local authority area by April 2006 and are the key mechanism for co-ordinating local safeguarding work. The Government is committed to a programme of action to support LSCBs and improve their effectiveness.

> ### Box 2.2: Local Safeguarding Children Boards
>
> The role of Local Safeguarding Children Boards role is to:
>
> - co-ordinate what is done by each person or body represented on the Board for the purposes of safeguarding and promoting the welfare of children in the area of each local authority; and
>
> - ensure the effectiveness of work to safeguard children and young people in the local area.
>
> Some local organisations have to be members of the LSCB by law, including local authorities, health services, police, probation, youth justice organisations and Connexions. Other partners such as schools, further education institutions, the NSPCC, and other voluntary and community sector bodies should be involved in the LSCB.

2.47 We need to ensure that concerns about children's welfare are picked up and acted on effectively by local authorities and their partners, to help children to get the protection and support they need.

2.48 In some instances families are not able to give children the support and protection they deserve without help from local services. In the great majority of cases, it should be the decision of parents when to ask for help and advice on their children's care and upbringing.

2.49 However, professionals do also need to engage parents early when doing so may prevent problems or difficulties becoming worse. In exceptional cases there remains a need for compulsory intervention in family life to safeguard children from significant harm. Children who suffer abuse or neglect within their families are extremely vulnerable and unlikely to have access to the love, stimulation and the stable environment they need to develop.

2.50 Safeguarding children and young people from harm, whatever the source of that harm may be, depends upon those who work with or encounter children being alert to, and acting on, signs and symptoms, including of abuse or neglect.

2.51 Effective communication and sharing of information are vital. Recording and communicating information in a clear and timely manner, and systematically gathering information from a range of sources, improves identification of children and young people in need or at risk of harm. Sharing of information in cases of concern about children's welfare will enable professionals to consider jointly how to proceed in the best interests of the child and to safeguard children more generally, and will inform effective assessments of children's needs. Supporting tools such as ContactPoint will play an important role in facilitating better communication between practitioners in different services.

2.52 A significant number of young people run away from home or care each year, putting themselves at significant risk of harm. Local authorities need to have services in place to intervene to prevent running away whenever possible, and to protect those who do run away as part of their broader responsibilities for safeguarding children and young people. A new indicator on the number of young people who run away from home or care has been included in the National Indicator Set (part of the new more focused but less bureaucratic arrangements for holding local areas accountable to local people and central government), demonstrating our commitment to improving services for young runaways. We asked The Children's Society to look at how services for young runaways could be improved, and are now working closely with them to consider and move forward their recommendations.

2.53 The voluntary sector has an important role to play and can provide children and young people with a wide range of services which contribute to children's safety, including:

"promoting wider awareness of safety, a range of wider activities that contribute to safety, and certain more specialist services" (voluntary sector organisation response to Staying Safe)

2.54 One of the clear messages from the *Staying Safe* consultation has been the need to do more to strengthen the role of the voluntary sector and the capacity of smaller voluntary sector organisations to engage fully in safeguarding. Several voluntary sector groups have raised concerns that they were unable to access training around child protection policies and safer recruitment in the same way as statutory services. This is an issue we will consider further in the *Staying Safe Action Plan.*

2.55 LSCBs are also ensuring that when a child has been killed or seriously harmed and abuse or neglect is suspected, steps are taken to learn the lessons and help prevent similar cases in the future by carrying out a comprehensive Serious Case Review.

2.56 In addition, from April 2008, each LSCB will put in place a Child Death Overview Panel (CDOP) which will take an overview of all child deaths (from birth, excluding stillborn babies, up to 18 years) in the local area. Neighbouring areas may share a CDOP.

2.57 We announced funding of £7.2 million in 2008–09, £7.4 million in 2009–10, and £7.7 million in 2010–11 for child death review processes as part of the local government settlement. The Department of Health has also identified the need to support the participation in these processes by health professionals over the same period. We will monitor the implementation of these new arrangements and the overall working of the child protection system.

Preventing unsuitable people from working with children

2.58 One of Government's main roles in safeguarding the young and vulnerable is to help prevent unsuitable people from gaining access to them through their work. It is employers' responsibility to follow safe recruitment and employment practices.

2.59 We have significantly strengthened systems to support safe recruitment by helping employers fulfil their responsibilities for checking the background of prospective staff. Regulations have been strengthened so that anyone cautioned or convicted for specified sexual offences against children will be automatically included on List 99 and barred from working in schools and other education or regulated childcare settings.

2.60 In addition, Criminal Records Bureau checks are now mandatory for all new appointments to the schools and early years workforce, including staff entering the profession from overseas, and we have published comprehensive guidance for education settings, *Safeguarding and Safer Recruitment in Education* which is underpinned by new regulations.

2.61 Through the Safeguarding Vulnerable Groups Act 2006, we have legislated to create the most robust scheme ever for vetting individuals who are applying to work with children and vulnerable adults, and for barring them where they are found to be unsuitable. **The new Independent Safeguarding Authority will be established in early 2008.**

> ### Box 2.3: The Independent Safeguarding Authority
>
> The Government is introducing the toughest ever vetting and barring scheme, designed to prevent those who are known to pose a risk of harm to children or vulnerable adults from gaining access to them through their work. The scheme, to be operated under the Safeguarding Vulnerable Groups Act, places new duties on employers and employees and is enforced through criminal law.
>
> Once the new scheme is introduced, all those seeking to work with children or vulnerable adults, in either a paid or unpaid capacity, will need to register with the Independent Safeguarding Authority before they enter the workforce. Employers, and those who manage the work of volunteers, must check that the individual is registered before he or she can start work.
>
> The Government is conducting a vigorous communications campaign to ensure that employers and stakeholders know and understand their new duties and responsibilities. For more information see www.isa-gov.org.uk.

2.62 All employers and stakeholders, including those in the voluntary sector, need to understand the implications of the new Independent Safeguarding Authority for their paid staff and volunteers. In response to views given in the *Staying Safe* consultation, **we will consider in the *Staying Safe Action Plan* how we can help voluntary sector organisations to practise safe recruitment and employment, as part of their wider excellent work in keeping children safe.**

Conclusions

2.63 This chapter has set out some of main work that Government will take forward to meet our vision of children being safe and able to enjoy happy, fulfilling childhoods. We will publish the *Staying Safe Action Plan* in early 2008, responding to the *Staying Safe* consultation and setting out in more detail an extensive programme of action to improve all children and young people's safety. In the following chapters we set out how we will raise attainment of children and narrow the gap in achievement between the most disadvantaged children and their peers.

Chapter 3: Excellence and equity

Individual progress to achieve world class standards and close the gap in educational achievement for children from disadvantaged families

Executive summary

3.1 We want every young person to achieve their potential and enjoy their time in education. Parents' support for their child's learning is an essential foundation for achievement. Parents told us they want to be more involved in their children's education, and schools see the benefits of greater engagement with parents. High quality early years education ensures that children are ready to succeed at school and is particularly beneficial to those from disadvantaged backgrounds. Our expert groups told us that the best way to achieve world class standards is a system in which all children receive teaching tailored to their needs and which is based on their 'stage not age'.

3.2 Partnership with parents is a unifying theme of the Children's Plan. Early years settings, primary schools and the best secondary schools have done much to work with parents and involve them in their child's education. However, we have further to go to deliver our vision for all parents, especially in secondary school, and so:

- we will set out and consult on a new relationship between parents and schools and legislate if necessary in order that:
  - parents will be contacted by a staff member at secondary school before their child starts at the school
  - parents will be able to attend information sessions at the new school
  - every child will have a personal tutor who knows them in the round, and as a main contact for parents
  - parents will have regular, up to date information on their child's attendance behaviour and progress in learning
  - Parents Councils will ensure that parents' voices are heard within the school; and
  - parents' complaints will be managed in a straightforward and open way

- we will spend £30 million over the next three years to provide more family learning to help parents and carers develop skills and learn with their children in schools.

3.3 Having created over the last decade a universal early years and childcare system, and having raised the entitlement to free early education and childcare for 3- and 4-year-olds from 12.5 to 15 hours a week, we will now invest £100 million over three years to:

- extend the offer of up to 15 hours of free early education and childcare to 20,000 2-year-olds in the most disadvantaged communities.

3.4 In schools, building on the £144 million already allocated over the next three years in the Every Child a Reader and Every Child Counts programmes to provide intensive support to children in primary schools at risk of falling behind, we will:

- allocate £25 million over the next three years to an Every Child a Writer programme to offer intensive one-to-one coaching in the areas of writing children find hardest to master;

- offer new 'age not stage' tests which children will take when they are ready and which, if current trials prove successful, will replace Key Stage tests at ages 11 and 14; and

- publish new indicators to show the performance of pupils achieving level 7 or above in English, mathematics and science and achieving level 8 and above in mathematics, to ensure proper attention is given to gifted and talented learners.

3.5 As our experts highlighted, the curriculum should help children move seamlessly from nurseries to schools, from primary to secondary and then to work or further and higher education. It should ensure all children secure the basics, while allowing flexibility to learn new skills and develop the social and emotional skills they need to succeed. Therefore we have announced a root and branch review of the Primary Curriculum, led by Sir Jim Rose, to ensure there is:

- more time for the basics so children achieve a good grounding in reading, writing and mathematics;

- greater flexibility for other subjects;

- time for primary school children to learn a modern foreign language; and

- a smoother transition from play-based learning in the early years into primary school, particularly to help summer-born children who can be at a disadvantage when they enter primary school.

3.6 In order to meet our 2020 goals for educational achievement, we will need to improve the attainment of some specific groups who we know are currently under-performing. Our vision is that there will be ready access from schools to the range of support services necessary to ensure barriers to learning are broken down. We will:

- spend £18 million over the next three years to improve quality of teaching for children with special educational needs, including:
  - better initial teacher training and continuous professional development;
  - better data for schools on how well children with Special Educational Needs are progressing; and
  - a pilot scheme in which children with dyslexia will receive Reading Recovery support or one-to-one tuition from specialist dyslexia teachers.

- ask Her Majesty's Chief Inspector of Schools to review progress on Special Educational Needs in 2009, in the light of the impact of greater personalised learning.

Vision for the next decade

3.7 To give every child the best start and allow them to realise their potential, the Government's vision for the next decade is to deliver universal high quality early childhood services to support each child's learning and development and give them solid foundations for later life. World class schools providing excellent, personalised teaching and learning will then help all children and young people – including the most disadvantaged and vulnerable – to progress in their education and wider development. At every stage, children and young people will have opportunities to grow and develop, and their individual needs will be addressed in the round by the complete range of children's services.

3.8 Over the last few years personalised learning has become increasingly widespread in both early years settings and in schools. Personalised learning puts children and their needs first. The Children's Plan sets out how we move to a more sophisticated approach to personalisation making it standard practice across the system. This new approach will look widely at all barriers to learning inside or outside the classroom faced by children and will, working collaboratively with other services, work to overcome them. This will realise the Government's aim that all children be supported to progress and no child should be left behind.

3.9 Building on the progress made over the last decade, we need to see faster rises in standards and to close the gaps in achievement that exist for disadvantaged and vulnerable children. Children from deprived backgrounds are three times less likely to achieve good outcomes at age 16. Children in care face particular barriers to their education and there are significant variations in the results achieved by children with special educational needs across the country.

3.10 The plans set out here for greater personalisation, supported by a more flexible and engaging curriculum, a workforce consistently at the level of the best and swifter intervention in failing and coasting schools will deliver our ambitions for 2020.

The ambition

3.11 World class early childhood services enable young children to have the best start in life so they can take full advantage of later opportunities to learn and develop. Therefore, the Government's ambition is that every child by age 5 will be developing well and ready to start their next phase of learning, having the confidence and communication skills to access the primary curriculum. **Our 2020 goal is that every child will be ready for success in school with at least 90 per cent developing well across all areas of the Early Years Foundation Stage Profile by age 5.** This will require us to build on the creation of a universal early years system, with a fresh impetus on improving quality, supporting parents and providing help earlier to those who need it most.

3.12 By age 11, all children should be ready for secondary school, and by 2020 our ambition is that **at least 90 per cent are achieving at or above the expected level in both English and mathematics**. Achieving this ambition will have a significant impact on attainment gaps and ensure that pupils from disadvantaged backgrounds start secondary school with the basics needed to progress well and provide a secure foundation for continued learning, underpinning our ambitions for young people to 18 and beyond set out in Chapter 5.

3.13 To drive progress toward these 2020 goals, we will focus on meeting the Public Service Agreement Government has agreed for 2011 to raise the educational achievement of all children and young people (PSA 10) (reflecting children and young people's development and educational attainment at the National Curriculum stages and levels, explained in detail in Annex D) measured by:

- the proportion of children reaching a good level of development at the end of the Early Years Foundation Stage;

- the proportion achieving Level 4 in both English and mathematics at Key Stage 2;

- the proportion achieving Level 5 in both English and mathematics at Key Stage 3; and

- the proportion achieving five A*–C GCSEs or equivalent including GCSEs in English and mathematics at Key Stage 4.

3.14 To ensure we also start to break the link between disadvantage and attainment, we have a second Public Service Agreement to narrow the gap in educational achievement between children from lower income and disadvantaged backgrounds and their peers (PSA 11).

3.15 Reinforcing our commitment that no child is left behind, statutory early years targets have been introduced for local authorities to improve more rapidly the levels of achievement of young children most at risk of falling into the lowest group. For later Key Stages national progression targets have been set alongside threshold targets. Schools have now been asked to improve the percentage of pupils moving two levels between Key Stages. The targets for 2011 will ensure that expected progress is maintained for *all* children and young people, including those who have previously fallen behind the most able measured by:

- the achievement gap between the lowest achieving 20 per cent of children and the rest at the end of the Early Years Foundation Stage;

- the achievement gap between pupils from low income families who are eligible for free school meals and their peers achieving the expected level at Key Stages 2 and 4;

- the proportion of pupils progressing by two levels in English and mathematics at each of Key Stages 2, 3 and 4;

- the proportion of children in care achieving Level 4 in English and mathematics at Key Stage 2; and

- the proportion of children in care achieving five A*–C GCSEs (or equivalent) at Key Stage 4.

Key areas for reform

3.16 Working in partnership with parents will be vital at each stage of children's development. Personalised teaching and learning will become the norm in every early years setting and classroom, stretching and challenging the able as well as ensuring no child falls behind.

3.17 A high quality early years system in which children learn through play, will build a firm foundation for learning. All children will then be motivated to learn in school by highly structured and responsive teaching, based on a detailed understanding of where pupils are in their learning, where they need to go, and how they will get there.

3.18 They will be supported by a flexible curriculum, offering opportunities to develop critical personal, social and emotional skills and develop the knowledge and understanding required to be active and responsible citizens.

3.19 Chapter 4 sets out how we will achieve a high quality early years and schools system to support this move to a personalised approach. This will involve the development of the workforce, creating the right environment for learning and driving improvements in each institution in the system. Again, this relies upon the collaborative relationship between schools, early years providers and the wide range of children's services.

Parents as partners in learning

3.20 Partnership with parents is a unifying theme of this Children's Plan. Our vision of 21st century children's services is that they should engage parents in all aspects of their children's development, and that children's services should be shaped by parents' views and command parents' confidence. While much progress has been made in Sure Start Children's Centres and primary schools, more needs to be done to reach out to and involve all parents particularly in secondary schools.

3.21 As the secondary phase approaches and when their children reach their teens, parents can feel more detached from their child's learning. Based on what we know about what is happening in some secondary schools and drawing on the struggle some parents have told us they face, we think the time is right to set out a new relationship with parents, no matter what their personal circumstances – mothers, fathers, non-resident parents, lone parents and working parents. We want to see parents experiencing all aspects of the good practice outlined below during their children's secondary education. We will now talk to schools, parents and young people and local authorities to see how rapidly we can achieve a system which could deliver on the commitments set out below.

3.22 The Government wants to see **parents contacted by a staff member at a secondary school before the child starts at the school**. All parents will benefit from an automated and transparent process when choosing a secondary school and for those parents who need help, local Choice Advisers will offer practical advice and support in navigating the admissions system. Parents will have access to information sessions as their child starts secondary school. Personalised learning will ensure that information about the child's academic progress and their personal development at primary school will be passed on to the secondary school to ensure continuity. The secondary school will check whether additional support is required, drawing on Parent Support Advisers, family support services and parenting support activities that will increasingly be available through extended schools.

3.23 From the moment they arrive in secondary school **every child will have a personal tutor who knows them well in the round and as a main contact for parent**. The tutor will coordinate support for the child involving the parent throughout their time in the school. They will help with induction, offering an introductory session before the child starts secondary school; agree learning targets term by term; encourage the child's ambitions (academic and otherwise); help the child make choices; and be the first point of call in times of trouble – talking to their parents about all of this. They will also identify and help to tackle barriers to success beyond the classroom. They will draw on support from others such as classroom teachers, Learning Mentors, Parent Support Advisers and lead professionals.

3.24 Every parent will **have regular, up to date information on their child's attendance, behaviour and progress in learning**. A school website will also offer information, such as school events calendar, health and lifestyle issues, behaviour information and access to blogs from experts to parents. Discussions between parents and schools will cover what is expected from the pupil and how the parent can support their child. Parents evenings and face-to-face discussions between parents and teachers will be held at times when working parents can attend.

3.25 **Parents complaints will be managed in straightforward and open way** and as many issues as possible will be resolved quickly. Parents, particularly those who may not be so readily engaged, will understand the route to follow when they have a complaint. We will review what more can be done to streamline and strengthen these arrangements

3.26 Governing bodies must listen and respond to the views of all parents, and this should include ensuring that fathers and working parents can participate fully. Every school will set out clearly the engagement and support parents can expect, and what opportunities and services are available if they need additional or targeted support. Schools will regularly seek the view of all parents, on issues such as the times and way that discussions with teachers can fit with their working patterns. **Parent Councils will ensure that parent's voices are heard within the school.** Extended schools will consult parents and the community about the opportunities, activities and services they provide, both as they start up and regularly thereafter.

3.27 Schools will spot early when a child has additional needs which are acting as a barrier to their learning. **The child's personal tutor will arrange additional support where that is needed to overcome barriers to learning.** The tutor will be able to draw support from other in-school professionals – such as the Parent Support Adviser, the SENCO or as part of targeted youth support services – and from a wider group of practitioners serving a cluster of schools. Together they will act as a 'team around the child', meet together to assess each child's needs and undertake a Common Assessment when necessary. The personal tutor will then agree with the team the action required and, if necessary, liaise with the lead professional, who will work directly with the child and their parents.

3.28 Through Parent Support Advisers and others, **schools will ensure that parents who find it more difficult are also involved** and will reach out to parents, including through community settings. They will encourage parents' involvement with their children's learning and support better behaviour and attendance, offer advice with parenting, and provide support for children and parents at the first sign the pupil may be experiencing social, health or behavioural issues.

3.29 Aspects of this vision exist in many schools, thanks to the dedicated efforts of school staff and the benefits of workforce reform. But for parents as a whole, this is a long way from being the common experience. We will seek parents' views on what are the priorities. We will talk to those schools that are leading exponents of engaging parents to see what valuable lessons they can offer others. We will also talk to local authorities to establish best practice in ensuring that specialist practitioners work seamlessly with the school in a 'team around the child' to intervene early and effectively. We will want schools and children's services to consider how they measure up against best practice, developing and sharing it at the local level. However, this may not be sufficient to make rapid progress, so we will consider in our discussions with parents and schools whether progress would be accelerated by more specific requirements, regulation or legislation.

3.30 The consultation has highlighted the secondary phase as worthy of specific, early attention, but we think the spirit behind these commitments apply to all stages of the system from early years, through primary and middle schools, all maintained secondary schools, including special schools, and all other children's settings.

3.31 Family Learning Programmes enable parents and carers to develop their skills and learn with their children. This includes the family literacy, language and numeracy programme which engages approximately 70,000 parents and carers per year and targets the most disadvantaged families. We know demand from parents outstrips the places available and has proved to be effective in raising parents' skills and qualification levels and employability. It has met parents' literacy, language and numeracy needs and given them the confidence to engage in their children's learning. Therefore, **we will allocate £30 million over the next three years to provide more family learning**.

The best start in the early years

3.32 Children's experience in the early years provides them with the foundation for success in later life. High quality early education helps to prevent gaps opening up between disadvantaged children and their more privileged peers. Since 1997, we have created a universal early years system. Use of regular, reliable care has benefits for children's development and benefits for parents – enabling them to consider training and work opportunities and making it easier for them to access wider family support services.

Box 3.1: Sure Start Children's Centres

Sure Start Children's Centres help to ensure children have the best start in life and to narrow the gap between the most disadvantaged children and their peers.

There are currently over 1,750 designated Sure Start Children's Centres offering services to over a million children and their families. By the end of 2008 there will be 2,500, covering all children and families in the 30 per cent most disadvantaged neighbourhoods. By 2010, there will be 3,500 across the country – a Sure Start Children's Centre for every community – with all centres providing all families with young children access to high quality early years services and other health and family support, as well as improved support for their children's transition into school. Centres in the most deprived areas will offer more intensive support and outreach services.

3.33 Although disadvantaged families often have most to gain from high quality early years provision, they are least able to afford it and may not wish to take it up. Quality of childcare and early education is still variable. Standards must become consistently excellent and be available to parents.

Personalisation supporting children's development

3.34 Every child is unique and will benefit most from an approach tailored to their needs. That approach will take into account children's different rates of progress and their different backgrounds and life experiences. Practitioners in good early years settings know what children can already do, what abilities they are developing, and how to extend their experiences to promote their development.

3.35 The best settings carry out observational assessment as part of their day to day work with children, which informs the support and encouragement practitioners offer to that child. However, high quality observational assessment is far from universally used, and as a result children can miss out on the help they need from adults.

3.36 To improve practice, we will offer tools that can be used by all settings to track children's development from the first time they start at an early learning and childcare setting. We will develop new tools and guidance to support assessment throughout the Early Years Foundation Stage (see Box 3.2). It should also help to strengthen assessment within and communication between settings about individual children, for example through the use of the Common Assessment Framework. This will improve the quality of the experiences children have in childcare and early education and reassure parents that their children's development is being supported.

The Early Years Foundation Stage

3.37 As set out in Box 3.2, the Early Years Foundation Stage is a clear framework of standards for all practitioners working in the early years. It reflects what good parents and carers do with their children – and is based firmly around a philosophy of play-based learning that supports all aspects of children's development.

Box 3.2: Personalisation in the early years – the Early Years Foundation Stage

The Early Years Foundation Stage (EYFS) provides a single framework for early learning and childcare. It sets out the level of cognitive, social, physical and personal development we want all children to reach by the age of 5. For the first time, the EYFS brings together early learning and care, recognising that we need to support children's development in the round and offer high quality play-based early learning that will allow children to achieve their full potential.

The EYFS, which comes into force in September 2008, is rooted in the philosophy of personalisation, and of helping children learn and develop at a pace which matches their unique needs. Rather than prescribe a fixed curriculum, the EYFS will set 'early learning goals', which recognise that children's development will proceed at different rates. This flexibility will allow providers to:

- tailor their approach to meet particular philosophies, giving parents greater choice about the environment in which their child learns;

- be flexible in adapting provision to fit the particular needs of individual children; and

- take into account the full range of the child's experiences over the course of a day, and for different forms of provision to complement one another.

Each child will also have a key person assigned to them who should plan to meet the needs of the child in their care, in partnership with parents.

3.38 However, children must be attending these high quality settings if they are to benefit from them – and so we must improve the access and the affordability of early years provision. In particular, we must improve outreach to those who would benefit, ensuring that they are aware of the support that is on offer to help them manage work and family life.

Access, affordability and availability

3.39 At present, every 3- and 4-year-old is entitled to at least 12.5 hours free early education each week, for 38 weeks a year. This is generally delivered in five sessions per week, but in some places is offered more flexibly to meet parents' needs. Take up is high, with 96 per cent of 3-year-olds and virtually all 4-year-olds taking up some provision. However, 40 per cent of children do not take up all of it, and there is a 15 per cent gap in take up levels between those in the highest and the lowest income quintiles.

3.40 We have already committed to **extend the free entitlement over the next three years to 2010–11 so that, by 2010, all children are entitled to 15 hours free early education per week**. Because we want services to be designed and delivered around the needs of families, the entitlement will be delivered more flexibly than at present. We know from the pilots currently taking place in 20 local authority areas that offering longer, more flexible provision improves take up. We will roll out the extended entitlement over the next three years, beginning with the most disadvantaged families.

3.41 We are also piloting free childcare for 12,000 disadvantaged 2-year-olds, and the pilot has led to more effective outreach and better communication between early years providers, local authorities and local parents. The pilots also include family support – an example of how services can work together to meet the needs of families.

3.42 Reflecting the success of the pilots, **over the next three years we will invest £100 million to extend the offer of up to 15 hours of free early years education and childcare places to 20,000 2-year-olds in the most disadvantaged communities**. This offer will be underpinned by activity to reach and support those families most in need, and as set out in Chapter 4, we will also target policies to continue to drive up the quality of childcare in these areas.

3.43 Beyond these free entitlements, the new Duty placed on local authorities by the Childcare Act to secure sufficient childcare for working parents and those wishing to work, will, from April 2008, improve the availability and flexibility of childcare provision in response to parents' needs. We expect that greater availability and accessibility will increase the take-up of formal childcare by disadvantaged families who have most to gain from work and whose children will benefit from high quality care, but who are most likely to be working atypical hours making it harder to find childcare.

3.44 We will continue, through advertising, PR and work with local authorities, Jobcentre Plus and health professionals, to spread more widely messages about the benefits, availability and affordability of childcare. We will work with HM Revenue & Customs (HMRC) to increase take-up of the childcare element of the Working Tax Credit and improve levels of understanding and trust amongst parents. Lessons from pilots in London to support childcare for parents training for work and those with a disabled child, will also contribute to improving the accessibility and affordability of childcare.

Reaching out to disadvantaged groups

3.45 Sure Start Local Programmes, and now Sure Start Children's Centres, include outreach and home visiting services to provide parents and carers at greatest risk of social exclusion with a gateway to the services their families need.

3.46 With some families establishing a relationship of trust takes time and dedicated effort. There have been significant successes, with families reporting they were glad to have taken new opportunities that had helped their children's wellbeing and had started parents on the road to greater self-reliance, training, and eventually employment.

3.47 But there is still a great deal to do. Too many children still miss out on services that could help them reach their full potential. We have therefore committed additional funding to support outreach activities with the most disadvantaged families, boosting the resources in Sure Start Children's Centres from next year, and enabling **local authorities to fund two outreach posts in Sure Start Children's Centres serving the most disadvantaged communities**. Visiting families at home has been shown to be one of the most effective ways of encouraging them to come to their local Centre and take advantage of what it has to offer.

3.48 We know that staff attitude and behaviour is critical to successful engagement with families – no family wants to feel they are being judged or patronised. Staff themselves need good skills and information as well as supervision from professionals in their multi-agency team. They need to be able to keep a clear focus on improving outcomes for children while at the same time building positive relationships with parents.

3.49 As the 0–7 Expert Group recommended, we will clarify what good 'outreach' work is, and what skills and training are needed to do it well. We will also ensure that staff involved in this important work have the right level of management support. **We will improve the quality of outreach work through training and development.**

3.50 Currently children in care are less likely than their peers to benefit from high quality early years provision. This needs to change. Following the passage of the Children and Young Persons Bill, we will introduce an expectation in care planning arrangements for children under 5 that the social worker will work with the carer and local authority to arrange high quality early years education, except where it is demonstrated not to be in the best interests of the child.

Smoothing transitions into school

3.51 The transfer from a pre-school setting into school, or the transition from the Early Years Foundation Stage in a reception class into the first year of Key Stage 1, can be a difficult time for young children. This is a period when children are developing fast and where changes in routines can be unsettling. The change can currently represent a sharp shift in style – with much more formal methods of teaching replacing a play-based environment.

3.52 Evidence shows it is best for children that there should not be a sudden change from a play-based to formal class-based curriculum or from a focus on all aspects of children's development to one primarily on the cognitive. Instead the shift in teaching style and content should be gradual and continue to reflect individual children's range of needs and growing maturity. Smoothing these transitions will benefit all children and allow each child to progress at a speed that best suits their needs while they are adjusting to their new environments was discussed by the 0–7 Expert Group. In order to achieve this:

- curriculum reform will ensure that the primary curriculum dovetails with the early years, smoothing the teaching experience and the coherence of the 0–7 phase;

- partnerships between early years providers and schools will help secure a better match of teaching styles to children's needs between birth and age 7, set out in Chapter 4;

- greater joint working between the early years and schools workforce will increase awareness of how children are progressing. **Key Stage 1 teachers and early years practitioners should look together at Early Years Foundation Stage Profile outcomes in order to plan effectively for the next phase of each child's learning**; and

- extended services in schools should help children and their parents cope with transitions, through family learning and through information sessions for parents at the beginning of primary and secondary phases.

3.53 In line with reforms to strengthen the regulation of all national assessments, including early years assessment, we intend to establish an independent regulator of exams and assessment (as set out in Chapter 5). At the end of the Early Years Foundation Stage, children's development is assessed – their Early Years Foundation Stage Profile – to inform the level and type of support that they require when moving to Year 1. Parents and the public are entitled to feel confident that information about outcomes is accurate. We will strengthen our work through the National Assessment Agency to ensure that the moderation of Foundation Stage Profile outcomes is robust and that all practitioners are supported to build an accurate picture of young children's learning and development. The National Assessment Agency will develop accredited training for moderators and we will roll it out nationally to improve the expertise and consistency of all local authority moderation.

Personalised teaching and learning to aid progression

3.54 In the best schools in the country, excellent classroom practice has already established a pedagogy and culture of personalised teaching and learning. Our new approach in schools – which looks at progression across stages – means we will focus on every pupil, in every year group, not just those at the end of key stages and in the middle of the ability range.

3.55 Our challenge is to ensure that this approach becomes the norm and that we secure better personal development and educational progress for all children. This will also be reflected in the reforms set out in Chapter 5 for 14- to 19-year-olds, giving young people greater choice over the options for learning that meet their different interests.

3.56 Teaching and learning is most effective where teachers are enthusiastic and knowledgeable and have the confidence to stand back and encourage pupils to become independent learners. Supporting this kind of high quality, engaging teaching has been the goal of the Primary and Secondary National Strategies, delivered through guidance and hands-on support to schools. This approach is working to improve standards.

Box 3.3: Personalised teaching and learning

The distinctive feature of the pedagogy of personalisation is the way it expects all pupils to reach or exceed expectations, fulfil early promise and develop latent potential. Personalised lessons are stretching for everyone. At the heart of personalisation is the expectation of **participation, fulfilment** and **success**. The hallmarks are ambitious objectives, challenging personal targets, rapid intervention to keep pupils on trajectory, and vigorous assessment to check and maintain progress. There are clear plans to support those who do not or cannot maintain trajectory.

Other key features include:

Talking to learn: Pupils are challenged to justify their answers by explaining their thinking.

Guided work: The teacher works with a small group to apply what has been learnt in the main part of the lesson.

Keeping up: Instead of retrospective catch-up, the first impulse of personalisation is to hold pupils in to the pace of learning.

Tracking for success: Effective teachers are continually updating what they know about each child's progress and using the information to plan next steps with precision. Tools such as Assessing Pupil Progress are used to track progress and to tell pupils how they can do better.

Planning for progression: In the past, progress meant getting through topics. Today it is about pupils progressing in their learning. The curriculum is constructed to deliver efficient steps of progression, helped by the National Strategies Frameworks.

Stimulating new talents: A range of cultural and social opportunities are on offer to help children to discover or develop new interests and talents.

Different paths to the same ends: The curriculum of the past was dominated by content coverage led by the teacher. Today we are building a curriculum around optimum progression for individual pupil learning. This means improving the way we tailor the curriculum for individual needs, and increasing choice.

3.57 As set out by the Teaching and Learning in 2020 Review Group, personalised learning must be:

- learner-centred and knowledge-centred – paying close attention to learners' knowledge, skills, understanding and attitudes, connecting learning to what children already know; and

- assessment-centred – using formative assessment (ongoing day to day and periodic assessment by teachers in the classroom) and summative assessment (more formal testing) to support learning, with learners and their teachers working together to monitor progress and identify the next steps.

3.58   In applying this approach universally, teachers will:

- quickly identify what additional support a child needs, and have the means to provide it through a range of intervention programmes;

- have a clear understanding of where each child is in their learning, where they need to be, and what they need to do to get there;

- have access to new tests (subject to positive evidence from the Making Good Progress pilots, set out in Box 3.4 below) that confirm their own assessments, and motivate children to focus on the next steps in their learning;

- do this within an accountability system that recognises the difference they are making to all children, across the whole ability spectrum;

- where there are wider barriers to learning requiring targeted support from children's services, arrange for the child to have a broader assessment using the Common Assessment Framework (CAF) and the support of the local multi-agency team, who will work with the school to provide a co-ordinated package of support; and

- be able to report regularly to parents on their child's progress.

3.59   We have already invested significantly in personalised learning and extended schools. This investment is designed to increase schools' capacity to adopt new teaching strategies and offer more small-group and one-to-one help where appropriate. We have announced **a further £1.2 billion over the next three years to support personalisation, including support for children with special educational needs, and support for one-to-one tuition**.

3.60   We are also currently piloting radical new approaches to stimulate, support, assess and measure pupil progress through the Making Good Progress pilot which began in September 2007, and will run for two years in over 450 primary and secondary schools (see Box 3.4). The pilot is carrying through some of the key recommendations of the Teaching and Learning in 2020 Review Group.

3.61   The pilot is aimed at improving ongoing assessment and tracking by teachers, with an offer of one-to-one tuition for pupils who are making slow progress. It is also trialling new single level tests, which pupils will take when they are ready, rather than – as they do now – at the end of key stages. Progression targets, proportions of children began in the pilot a year earlier and now apply to all schools. This means that the achievement of all pupils matters not just those on the threshold borderline. We are piloting a financial premium as an incentive to schools to move on pupils two levels who have entered the Key Stage behind national expectations.

Box 3.4: Making Good Progress – the impact of personalised learning

The Making Good Progress pilot aims to improve rates of progression by focusing teachers, pupils and parents on the progress that each child makes term on term and year on year. Every pupil, regardless of their starting point, will count towards the schools' progression target to improve the proportion of pupils making two National Curriculum levels of progress throughout a Key Stage.

The pilot will place a greater emphasis on teachers' own assessments of where each pupil is in their learning and what the next steps should be. This will enable schools, teachers, parents and pupils to monitor termly the progress that each child makes. This continual feedback on performance will enable schools to target and intervene early – and will inform better reporting to parents.

Where a teacher believes that a pupil has progressed and is securely at the next National Curriculum level they will be able to enter them for a single level test to confirm that assessment: celebrating that pupil's progress and motivating parents, pupils and teachers to keep on reaching for the next level.

Teachers use their detailed knowledge of each pupil's progress to provide more accurate support, more differentiated teaching and more personal provision. For example, they adapt their teaching plans, re-group pupils in class according to their understanding, provide additional time and support on difficult topics, offer options and specialisms, set more challenging tasks for those who need to be stretched, and set personalised targets.

Where pupils begin to fall behind, swift, targeted support such as one-to-one tuition will enable them to 'keep up' with their peers rather than having to 'catch up', and will re-engage children in their learning, boosting their confidence.

3.62 Personalised practice can also help engage parents in their children's learning. Teachers can give better assessment data to parents, on a more regular basis and can discuss additional support where that is needed. This is critical to driving up standards. The policies to do this are set out below.

Assessment for learning

3.63 Assessment for Learning (AfL) practices such as target-setting, pupil self-assessment and peer assessment have been adopted by three quarters of schools. However, there is clear evidence that pupil assessment and the use of assessment in planning teaching remains the weakest aspect of teaching and learning in schools – but it is also one of the aspects which can make the most difference to children's achievement.

3.64 Our aim is to make the use of tracking and AfL tools and techniques truly universal across all schools – extending them beyond the core subjects of English and mathematics. This requires each school to have experts in assessment and intervention teaching who can support their colleagues.

3.65 We have already committed to **invest £150 million over the next three years in the continuing professional development of school staff in AfL**. The English and mathematics Assessing Pupil Progress materials, already developed by the Qualifications and Curriculum Authority, should become universally used in schools. We also want to expand those tools into more subjects, starting with Science.

Single level tests

3.66 The Making Good Progress pilots are evaluating the use of single level tests. These tests are shorter than the current end of Key Stage tests (see Annex D for a description of the Key Stages), and each cover a single level of the National Curriculum in reading, writing and mathematics, from Level 3 to Level 8. They are aimed at pupils from age 7 to age 14. The pilot schools have two opportunities a year to enter pupils, as soon as teachers believe they are ready to move on to the next level. Recommendations of the Expert Groups support this 'stage not age' approach to educational progress.

3.67 The tests are designed to motivate pupils and teachers by focusing them on achieving the next step in their learning throughout the Key Stage, rather than just at the end point. Because entry for the tests also depends on teacher assessment judgements, they aim to strengthen the relationship between ongoing teacher assessment, and formal testing. And because pupils are entered when they are ready, pupils are much more likely to experience success – those that do not can be entered again. We know from the *Time to Talk* consultation that parents and children feel concerned about end of Key Stage tests. This new approach should make the test experience feel less 'high stakes' for pupils, as well as contributing to better teaching and learning. We will also be able to use the tests in the same way as existing National Curriculum tests to hold schools accountable for the performance of children by the end of Key Stages and to ensure that parents can see the performance of their children's schools in the performance tables.

3.68 **It is our intention to implement new single level tests in reading, writing and mathematics on a national basis at the earliest opportunity, subject to positive evidence from the pilot and to endorsement of this approach from the Regulator. The new tests would replace the current National Curriculum tests for 11- and 14-year-olds.** We will also explore new options for the assessment of science. In the meantime, the current National Curriculum tests for science will continue.

Good classroom practices – better use of grouping and setting

3.69 Improved understanding of each child's progress should also lead to more effective use of group teaching. Since 1997 we have been encouraging schools to use 'setting' (teaching groups of pupils by ability in a *particular* subject rather than across a range of subjects) and other forms of pupil grouping, and we continue to encourage these practices.

3.70 Using setting and groups to teach children of similar abilities and interests can bring real educational benefits. But where it is poorly implemented, for example through 'streaming' (where pupils are grouped across a range of subjects based on general rather than subject-specific assessment) it can be socially divisive and detrimental to all but the highest achieving pupils. Grouping can also be used more effectively in the classroom – in particular, through proven approaches to in-class grouping by need, and guided group work when the teacher coaches a small group to apply immediately what they have been learning in the main part of the lesson. We will promote this best practice as standard practice.

Targeted support to keep up

3.71 A personalised approach also enables us to identify and intervene quickly where pupils are not progressing as they should. This allows pupils to 'keep up' rather than having to 'catch up' with their classmates, which is more difficult to do. Our ambition over the next ten years is that all children falling behind and failing to make sufficient progress should have additional support. As set out in Box 3.5 the Government has already introduced a number of targeted programmes to help children and young people in key areas in which they are struggling at school.

3.72 In addition, there will be a widespread expansion of one-to-one tuition so that all children have the support that in the past has been the preserve of those who can afford to pay for it. The Making Good Progress pilot provides up to ten hours of targeted one-to-one tuition in reading, writing and/or mathematics for 7–14-year-olds who are falling behind. Tuition takes place outside of the school day and is targeted at the pupil's specific needs as identified by their class teacher. Lessons learned from the pilot will inform the design of a wider individual tuition programme that will support 300,000 pupils a year in each of English and mathematics by 2010/11. Building on the success of one-to-one support for reading and mathematics, **we will allocate £25 million over the next three years to the Every Child a Writer programme offering intensive one-to-one coaching in the areas of writing children find hardest to master.**

3.73 We have also already committed to make funding available in 2009–10 and 2010–11 to **offer every young person in around a quarter of secondary schools an hour a week after school of academic-focused study support**. This will complement the varied menu of activities and study support element of the extended schools core offer.

Box 3.5: Personal support to catch up

In addition to the one-to-one tuition for pupils in Key Stages 2 and 3, now being piloted in the Making Good Progress schools, we are introducing three national support programmes to ensure that primary school children who struggle in the basics are equipped for secondary school.

Every Child a Reader (ECAR) places highly skilled teachers into primary schools to provide intensive one-to-one and small group support for those young children with the greatest difficulties in learning to read. ECAR will be rolled out nationally over the next three years following successful pilots, benefiting 30,000 children with severe literacy difficulties by 2010–11.

Every Child Counts, set to start in 2010, will be aimed at children whose attainment in mathematics as 6-year-olds shows they are failing to make expected progress for their age. Pupils will get intensive support each day from teachers, mostly provided one-to-one, but also through group work. It will reach approximately 30,000 6-year-old children by 2011.

Every Child a Writer will help children to express themselves in writing. The programme, which is still under development, will include one-to-one coaching in the areas of writing which children find the hardest to master. Every Child A Writer may offer support later in primary school than Every Child a Reader and Every Child Counts, which are targeted at younger primary school children, potentially reaching a greater number of pupils and teachers.

At secondary school we are rolling out the successful Study Plus pilot. **Study Plus** offers support within the school day to those pupils at Key Stage 4 who need additional support to achieve a good grasp of literacy and numeracy skills. In the 2006/07 pilot, the over-whelming majority of local authorities taking part reported improvements in the quality of Study Plus pupils' learning – noting higher levels of motivation and engagement, pupils being more confident and positive as learners. Teachers firmly expected that it would result in higher than anticipated attainment for targeted groups.

Personal support for every pupil

3.74 The Children's Plan sets out our commitment to ensuring that services consider the needs of children across all aspects of their lives and tailor provision to those needs. The Teaching and Learning in 2020 Review Group recommended that all secondary school pupils should have at least one person in school who knows them in the round – a personal tutor – both about their academic progress across all subjects, and their personal development – in the same way that a primary school teacher would for children in his or her class.

3.75 To support our Children's Plan vision, we want every secondary school pupil to have access to a single member of staff to play this role. The personal tutor will be familiar with each pupil's progress across all of their subject areas, agree learning targets across the curriculum, help children make subject choices, support them through transitions between stages of learning, and identify children's barriers to success beyond the classroom. The personal tutor will also have a key role in communicating with parents to report on their child's progress and discuss the support they need at home and at school.

3.76 As we develop the role of the personal tutor, we will also explore how they can help young people choose from a range of activities available through extended schools, in which they may want to participate to develop their talents, and will help young people to look forward to future education, training and career choices.

3.77 The personal tutor will build on the roles of many existing members of staff, including form tutors, pastoral staff, and learning mentors. We will establish a range of tested delivery models that schools can adopt by piloting this approach throughout 2008 and 2009, so that all schools can have personal tutors in place in 2010.

Effective transfer and transitions during school years

3.78 There is a particular risk of children's learning stalling when they transfer from primary school to secondary schools. That may be because of abrupt changes in curriculum or teaching styles, because children are emotionally or socially unprepared for the change; or because of simple administrative barriers to the transfer of information about individual children. The reforms set out in the Children's Plan will help ensure that the change to secondary school is as seamless as possible, as part of our vision that services should be consistently designed around children and families' needs.

3.79 The move to greater personalised learning will help to identify and prioritise those pupils who are in danger of stalling in their learning at the start of secondary school. It will also make much richer information on individual children's academic achievement at primary school available to secondary schools. Our new focus on supporting the development of children's social and emotional skills will help them to develop greater resilience and preparedness for change, both in learning, and socially.

3.80 The introduction of personal tutors will allow schools to strengthen the individual support available to pupils, and their parents, as they reach Year 7. We will explore the opportunity for parents to be offered an introductory session with their child's future learning guide, before their child starts secondary school, establishing before entry whether additional support may be required. This will involve Parent Support Advisers.

An inspiring and engaging curriculum

3.81 The school curriculum represents the classroom learning experience that each school provides for children. The aim of the curriculum is to develop the knowledge, understanding, skills and attitudes which are necessary for each pupil's self-fulfilment and development as an active and responsible citizen at each stage of their education. It prepares young people for further study, employment and adult life. It makes expectations for learning and attainment explicit to pupils, parents, teachers, governors, employers and the public, and establishes national standards for the performance of all pupils in the subjects it covers.

3.82 The National Curriculum core subjects are English, mathematics and science, which are the building blocks of a good education. In addition, all young people are entitled to a broad and rich curriculum, including access to high quality provision in the arts, music, languages and sport. The National Curriculum has enough flexibility to allow schools to build in the distinctive strengths of the school without losing focus on the vital areas of literacy and numeracy – and the best schools already take advantage of this curriculum.

Primary curriculum

3.83 As highlighted by the 0–7 Expert Group, the curriculum should support children's seamless experience of education between phases. While there have been significant recent curriculum changes, with the introduction of the Early Years Foundation Stage and the new secondary curriculum, the primary curriculum has remained largely unchanged since 2000. **Therefore we have announced a root and branch review of the primary curriculum to ensure continuity with the other phases. It will begin in spring 2008 and report back to the Secretary of State by March 2009 so that agreed changes to the curriculum can be implemented in September 2011.**

3.84 This will be the most fundamental review of the primary curriculum for a decade. It will establish the essential knowledge, skills and understanding our schools will teach all our primary aged pupils for years to come. It is important that a review of such significance seeks the views of a wide range of interested stakeholders and acknowledged experts in primary education. **The Government has appointed Sir Jim Rose, former Deputy Chief Inspector of Schools, member of the Qualifications and Curriculum Authority's Board, and author of the 2006 report into the teaching of early reading, to lead an independent Review of the Primary Curriculum.** He will be closely supported by the Qualifications and Curriculum Authority who will take the leading role in providing the evidence required for the review, and who will manage the associated consultations.

3.85 The review will create space to better personalise teaching and learning, whilst ensuring an excellent grounding in the basics. The review will build on Sir Jim Rose's review of the importance of phonics in teaching children to read, and on Sir Peter Williams' review of primary mathematics which is due to report in summer 2008. The review will also draw on an international benchmarking study, which the DCSF has commissioned of the primary curriculum in leading developed countries to ensure that our approach is world-class.

3.86 The review will seek to raise standards for all pupils by:

- providing greater continuity between the EYFS and Key Stage 1, and between Key Stage 2 and Key Stage 3;

- facilitating greater flexibility to narrow the attainment gap between disadvantaged pupils and their peers;

- continuing the strong focus on literacy, numeracy, scientific understanding, and the effective use of ICT;

- reducing prescription where possible to ensure that the primary curriculum allows all pupils the time they need to build on prior learning;

- ensuring all pupils have the time and space they need to make expected levels of progress in literacy and numeracy. It will consider how to ensure that that applies to summer-born children as much as their autumn-born peers;

- examining how best to introduce languages as a compulsory subject in Key Stage 2, as recommended by Lord Dearing;

- introducing children to the key ideas and practice of the other principal subject areas of learning – science and technology; the creative arts; the humanities; PE and sport – as a preparation for further learning at the secondary stage;

- securing pupils' personal, moral, social and emotional development through a more coherent and integrated curriculum framework, which also reflects the Every Child Matters outcomes; and

- creating more opportunities for pupils to experience more learning outside the classroom, through extended schools.

Personal development

3.87 One of the messages from the *Time to Talk* consultation was that children need to be treated more as individuals and not simply looked at in terms of attainment levels. Personal, social and emotional capabilities are closely related to educational attainment, success in the labour market, and to children's wellbeing. Developing these skills raises children and young people's confidence and aspirations about what they can achieve. Evidence also suggests that these 'softer' skills are becoming more important over time as the challenges facing young people get more complex. We will use the opportunity of the primary curriculum review to build on the work of the Early Years Foundation Stage to develop children's personal, social and emotional skills.

3.88 Personal development in primary schools has recently been enhanced by the Social and Emotional Aspects of Learning (SEAL) programme which offers a whole-school approach to developing social and emotional skills. SEAL helps schools create the climate and conditions which promote the development of these skills including activities to engage parents. The SEAL programme is currently used by around 60 per cent of primary schools. A phased roll-out of SEAL to secondary schools began in September 2007.

3.89 Personal development is also addressed through the National Healthy Schools Programme. Schools with National Healthy School Status will provide their pupils with the skills, understanding and attitudes to make informed decisions through personal, social and health education, healthy eating, physical activity, and emotional health and wellbeing. Our ambition is for all schools to work towards achieving National Healthy School Status by 2009, as set out in Chapter 1.

3.90 The 8–13 Expert Group called for a greater recognition of 'soft' skills in the curriculum and more work is needed to encourage schools to focus on children's personal development. We therefore propose that **the Review of the Primary Curriculum should consider how to develop a more integrated and simpler framework of the personal development skills which all pupils should expect to develop through their schooling.**

3.91 As set out in Chapter 1 we will consider how we might provide a record of children's personal development as they progress through primary school and beyond. A primary profile, recording a wider range of achievements, including personal development and achievement in foreign languages, sport and creative activities, would help parents follow their children's progress and would provide useful information for secondary schools and help aid transition.

3.92 Building on the new accountability structures set out in the Introduction and in Chapter 7, we will review with Ofsted the scope for strengthening the extent to which the assessment and accountability framework gives recognition to schools' performance in this area.

Skills for the 21st century

3.93 Alongside essential subject knowledge, the new secondary curriculum places a strong emphasis on the development of skills for life and work. As the Teaching and Learning in 2020 Review Group made clear, schools need to develop the skills that employers particularly value in their employees, such as good oral communication skills, reliability, punctuality and perseverance, the ability to work as part of a team, and the ability to work independently without close supervision. These essential skills and concepts are embedded throughout the new secondary curriculum.

3.94 Young people also need to develop the ability to think and act creatively and be innovative. As the Roberts Review *Nurturing Creativity in Young People* noted, creativity will be key to young people achieving economic wellbeing in adult life because of the increasing importance of the creative industries. These industries already account for over 7 per cent of the UK economy and are growing at almost twice the rate of the rest of the economy.

Secondary curriculum

3.95 A review of the secondary curriculum has just been completed for implementation from September 2008. We have freed up a significant proportion of the school day so that teachers will have more time to provide pupils with the additional support they need to progress. This will raise standards by creating additional flexibility and space for schools to help those students who have fallen below the expected level in English and mathematics. It will also allow more time for students to study areas in greater depth and to be set more challenging tasks. It will also mean that young people leave school with a sound knowledge of British history and with strong personal and social capabilities.

A cohesive society

3.96 Schools are well placed to become a focal point for the local community and to foster better relationships between diverse communities. The introduction of the duty on schools to promote community cohesion recognises the good work that many schools are already doing to encourage community cohesion and aims to achieve a situation where children:

- understand others, value diversity, apply and defend human rights and are skilled in participation and responsible action;

- fulfil their potential and succeed at the highest level possible, with no barriers to access and participation in learning and to wider activities, and no variation between outcomes for different groups; and

- have real and positive relationships with people from different backgrounds, and feel part of a community, at a local, national and international level.

3.97 The curriculum can play a key part in promoting community cohesion. Citizenship education, history, geography, religious education and personal, social and health education can all help young people develop a sense of identity. Links between different schools, whether on a local, national or international basis enable sharing of experience – contributing significantly to schools meeting the new duty.

3.98 Citizenship education addresses issues relating to social justice, human rights, community cohesion and global interdependence. The new citizenship programmes of study include a new strand of work examining the key concepts of identity and diversity and encouraging exploration of what it means to be a citizen in the UK today. This change was supported by the findings of the Review of Citizenship and Diversity in the Curriculum, undertaken by Sir Keith Ajegbo. Taking on board the advice of the Youth Citizenship Commission, we will consider what more needs to be done to improve the teaching of citizenship in our schools.

3.99 The London Olympic and Paralympic Games in 2012 offer a great opportunity to motivate more young people, and we will use the hosting of the Games to create an enduring educational and aspirational legacy to accelerate improvements in sport, the arts, language learning, sustainability, and citizenship education.

3.100 All of our secondary curriculum reforms are aimed at providing a more personalised, flexible and engaging curriculum which supports the needs of children and young people. With more ways to demonstrate progress and more pathways to choose from at Key Stage 4 (such as new Diplomas), learners will be far more likely to find something that motivates them so they can continue learning for longer and gain the qualifications they need to progress into further and higher education (discussed in Chapter 5).

Expanding opportunities through extended schools

3.101 Beyond the classroom, children and young people need to experience a wide range of activities. The Expert Groups and the *Time to Talk* consultation both emphasised to us how important it is for children to enjoy their childhood and develop their own talents. The implementation of extended schools provides the opportunity to help make this a reality. But we recognise that we need to support schools to offer this wider range of activities, especially in sport and culture.

Box 3.6: Extended schools

By 2010 all schools will be providing access to a range of extended services: a varied menu of activities, combined with childcare in primary schools; parenting support; swift and easy referral to targeted and specialist services, and wider community access to ICT, sports and arts facilities, including adult learning. The Government has invested £680 million to deliver this vision, and we have committed **a further £1.3 billion over the next three years**.

Evidence shows this approach is working. The recent evaluation of full service extended schools found positive impacts on pupil attainment and life chances, pupil engagement with learning, and on wider family stability. Children and young people also experienced positive personal, social and health outcomes. Overall, the impact was strongest for disadvantaged children, young people and families.

Extended schools are helping to make personalised learning real. Through their core offer extended schools deliver a coherent package of support to children and young people. This includes a focus on a wide variety of opportunities for learning beyond the classroom, making full use of other providers within the community.

Schools are encouraged to consult with children and young people and their parents on designing programmes of activities to help increase engagement with learning, offer new opportunities not otherwise available to many children and help stretch higher achievers – and are required by law to involve disabled children. In addition, through new support mechanisms, schools will be better able to help address individual barriers to learning.

Tackling deprivation and disadvantage to reduce attainment gaps is a core focus of extended schools. We are providing significant targeted funding to support the provision of academic study support in around a quarter of secondary schools. We have already announced that we are making £265 million available by 2010-11 to help schools provide and commission an exciting range of activities for children and young people.

This funding will help subsidise access to these opportunities by disadvantaged children, young people and children in care, who through their economic circumstances would otherwise be unable to participate. The funding will give schools the confidence to focus on providing what would most benefit children and young people, not just limited to what they can afford to pay for.

3.102 Major investment has meant that 86 per cent of primary and secondary school children now participate in at least two hours of PE and sport each week. We will ensure that by 2011 all 5–16-year-olds also have the opportunity to participate in an additional three hours of sporting activity either within or outside school; and that this three hour offer also applies to young people aged 16–19. We will also put an increasing emphasis on competition and coaching and improve facilities for disabled children and those with special educational needs.

3.103 Participation in cultural activity is enriching and contributes to the Every Child Matters outcomes. We recently announced a major school music programme and will now look to go further across a wider range of cultural activities. We will work towards a position where, no matter where they live, or what their background is, all children and young people can get involved in high quality cultural activities in and out of school, beginning with the piloted cultural offer set out in Chapter 5.

Tackling underachievement in specific groups

3.104 We are committed to narrowing, and ultimately closing, the gap between the progress and attainment of children from disadvantaged backgrounds and their peers. At present, a child from a low income family is three times less likely than average to achieve good results at age 16.

3.105 Personalised learning should have a significant impact on narrowing achievement gaps where they exist. As schools become increasingly sophisticated in making judgements about pupils' progress in the classroom, and using assessment data to track pupils, they should be able to use this information to identify where there are barriers beyond the classroom that need to be addressed. Poor educational progress may well be an indicator that a child is experiencing wider difficulties, for example at home or with health conditions.

3.106 Our new emphasis on ensuring all schools are contributing to and can rely on local Children's Trusts, set out in the Introduction and in Chapter 7, means that those who need it can access wider sources of help. Where schools can address barriers to learning through their own services they should do so, working with the full range of extended services already on offer to children and families. Where a more formal assessment is required to identify the barriers, or where multi-agency services are likely to be required, the school should complete a wider assessment using the Common Assessment Framework.

3.107 Additional support should then be available in the form of a local multi-agency 'team around the child'. Such teams should bring together, or provide ready access to, professionals from child health services, Child and Adolescent Mental Health Services, behavioural support and educational psychology services, speech and language therapy, family support (including parenting), educational welfare, social care and (for secondary schools) youth services and crime prevention. This kind of joined up support is essential to tackling major barriers to learning.

Box 3.7: Home Access Taskforce

There are significant educational benefits associated with having access to technology at home. This availability of technology gives learners greater choice about where, when and how they study. Research shows that this helps to motivate learners and improve attainment. We also know that learning technologies in the home can serve as a focal point for parents to become more actively involved in their child's education. This collaboration between learner and parent can further enhance a pupil's engagement and their achievement.

The Home Access Taskforce is investigating how to make sure that every learner has access to technology at home. The Taskforce will make recommendations in April 2008 detailing how universal access could be achieved. At the moment, there are over a million children with no access to a computer in the home. These children are disproportionately from disadvantaged backgrounds, and their limited access to technology reinforces attainment gaps.

3.108 Some black and minority ethnic groups are disproportionately more likely to be disadvantaged and on average achieve lower results at school. Black Caribbean, Black African and other Black pupils, those of Mixed White and Black Caribbean heritage, Bangladeshi and Pakistani pupils perform below the national average at all Key Stages.

3.109 However, the gap between average results for White British pupils and almost all of the other minority ethnic groups has been narrowing. If results are considered after taking into account deprivation and prior attainment, most ethnic minority groups make more progress than those pupils identified as White British. Children from some previously under attaining groups have caught up – for example, Bangladeshi pupils' performance now almost equals that of the whole school population – and Black pupils are improving twice as fast as other pupils.

3.110 There are pockets of under attainment, as well as some gender imbalances, within minority ethnic groups. We will continue to monitor closely the interaction between disadvantage, ethnicity and other social and environmental influences on children's progress and attainment. *Reach*, an independent report commissioned by the Government, was published in August 2007, and made five recommendations on measures that could improve the attainment and aspirations of Black boys and young Black men. In December 2007 the Government responded to those recommendations, and we will be working closely with other government departments to take forward the relevant recommendations.

3.111 Some children also lack the language skills to make good progress at school. For children for whom English is an additional language (EAL), we already provide a major programme of support at school and community level. Dedicated funding and resources available for this purpose have kept pace with patterns of migration. The evidence shows that EAL children typically catch up with their peers within two years.

Children with special educational needs and disabled children

3.112 Almost a fifth of children are identified as having special educational needs (SEN), which means they have a learning difficulty that calls for additional or different provision than that made for other children. This will include most disabled children who have a specific impairment which affects their ability to carry out everyday activities. There is a significant overlap between disabled children and those with SEN. Many of these children are successfully included in mainstream schools. Some children with a range of complex needs and profound learning disabilities are taught in special schools.

3.113 The focus on attainment of vulnerable groups, particularly those with SEN, was recognised as a key issue by the 8–13 Expert Group. Government wants to ensure that every child with SEN gets an education that allows them to achieve their full potential. The Disability Discrimination Act and the Disability Equality Duty require every local authority and school to ensure that disabled children are able to access all aspects of the curriculum.

3.114 Personalised teaching and learning approaches will help us deliver improved outcomes for all children, including children with SEN, enabling us to achieve our 2020 goals, set out in the Introduction. However, many children with SEN will require additional specialist support. Mainstream schools can and should be providing high quality support for the vast majority of these children. Working collaboratively with specially resourced provision, with support services and special schools, mainstream schools can ensure that the wide spectrum of SEN is met. There is a continued commitment to special school provision, most of which will be rebuilt or refurbished by 2020.

3.115 New indicators on the gap between the attainment of children with SEN and their peers mean that, for the first time, government will be held to account explicitly for the progress made by children and young people with SEN. Furthermore, the progress of children with SEN is critical to the achievement of our 2020 ambitions. Children and young people themselves, their parents, and the professionals who work with them, must have the highest aspirations for each child. In turn, government's responsibility is to support them by putting in place the required policies and structures.

3.116 Where it works well, the SEN framework ensures early identification of children's needs; a strong voice for the child and parents in their education; close co-operation between all agencies involved; and full access to the curriculum. However, in some cases identifying a child as having SEN can also lead to low expectations – an excuse for a widening gap with their peers, rather than a means to secure the support that enables them to catch up.

3.117 We recognise that more needs to be done to improve outcomes and provision for children with SEN and disabled children to increase parental confidence that children's individual needs are being met. Over the next three years, we will spend £18 millon to:

- improve the workforce's knowledge, skills and understanding of SEN and disability **through better initial teacher training and continuing professional development** by working with the Training and Development Agency for Schools and others. In initial teacher training, we want providers to offer specialist units on SEN and disability, which have been successfully piloted. For new teachers' induction, we will promote further use of specialist materials and look for opportunities to extend and strengthen the knowledge and skills of newly qualified teachers as they take up posts in schools. We will also invest further in the Inclusion Development Programme (IDP), which aims to increase the skills of the whole early years and school workforce in dealing with children with speech, language and communication needs and dyslexia; autistic spectrum disorders; and behavioural, emotional and social difficulties. We will continue to work with key voluntary sector partners to develop specialist trusts in relation to dyslexia, communication needs and autism, which will encourage teachers to become specialists in these important areas;

- **better data for schools on how well children with special educational needs are progressing.** Professionals need better information to understand what constitutes good progress for children identified with different types of educational needs, which can also form the basis of evidence-based discussions, support and challenge about each school's performance in this area with Ofsted and School Improvement Partners;

- continue to strengthen the position of the SEN co-ordinator in schools, including consulting on regulations requiring them to be teachers and working towards the introduction of nationally accredited training arrangements for all those new to the role;

- **a pilot scheme in which children with dyslexia will receive Reading Recovery Support or one-to-one tuition from specialist dyslexia teachers**. As we have recently announced, **we will also be providing additional funding to the British Dyslexia Association to enable them to provide information and advice for teachers and parents on best practice in identifying and supporting children with dyslexia**; and

- address factors that hold back the progress of children with SEN and disabled children, in particular bullying and high levels of exclusion.

3.118 The Bercow Review into the provision of services for children and young people with speech, language and communication needs was launched in September 2007. The Review will consider improving information to parents to help identify issues early and encourage them to seek support; improve the skills of the early years and school workforce; promote better partnership working between health and local authority services; and ensure clear accountability in all services. In spring 2008 it will publish its interim report, reflecting the outcomes of its consultation, with a final report in summer 2008.

3.119 Through regular contact with local authorities and the work of the SEN Advisers Team in the National Strategies we will continue to support and challenge local authorities to improve the operation of the SEN framework in their area. We recognise that parental confidence in the system for assessing and providing statements of SEN needs to be increased.

3.120 We will undertake research to look at the experience of parents through the process of school and local authority assessment of their child's needs and the provision of a statement, where necessary, to identify how schools, local authorities and the SEN and Disability Tribunal can work better together to improve processes.

3.121 We will also be publishing shortly our response to the Education and Skills Select Committee report on the separation of the role of local authorities in the assessment and funding of children with a statement of SEN.

3.122 Our reforms in *Aiming high for disabled children*, should help ensure the needs of disabled children are better met (this is set out in more detail in Chapter 1). Over the coming year, we will have stronger evidence of effective school practice on personalised learning and progression; the additional investment in workforce skills will begin to make an impact; and the Disability Equality Duty on schools should be making a practical difference to the inclusion of disabled children. **We will ask Her Majesty's Chief Inspector of Schools to review progress on special educational needs in 2009, in the light of the impact of greater personalised learning.** This review will include looking at how well the needs of disabled children are being met.

Children in care

3.123 As set out in *Children and Young People Today*, in 2006, only 12 per cent of those in care achieved five A*–C at GCSE (or equivalent) compared to 59 per cent of all children. Outcomes for this vulnerable group of children and young people are unacceptable and, despite improvements, insufficient progress has been made. Children in care were recognised as a group with particular needs by all three Expert Groups.

3.124 *Care Matters: Time for Change*, published in June 2007, set out a detailed programme of work to improve the education of children in care. This is consistent with the Children's Plan vision of a system which supports the needs of individual children. It will improve their access to quality early education, priority in school admissions and personalised support at school and we are:

- increasing the importance of education in care proceedings, including improving the stability of children in care's education by restricting school moves caused by care planning;

- introducing 'virtual school heads' who, at a local authority level, will be responsible for improving the attainment of children and young people in care and will provide support and challenge to schools;

- putting the role of a designated teacher for children in care on a statutory footing to ensure that the barriers to their learning are tackled; and

- providing an annual educational allowance of £500 for all children in care at risk of falling behind to enable them to access wider provision such as further one-to-one support outside of school or positive activities which support their education.

3.125 The Children and Young Persons Bill, currently before the House of Lords, provides the legislative framework for this change. As highlighted in Chapter 1, in the New Year, we will publish further details of the implementation of *Care Matters* setting out how we will build on the momentum of the change for children in care.

Helping summer-born children

3.126 Summer-born children are up to a year younger than their classmates when they sit tests at the end of each Key Stage. This affects their performance right through school up to the age of 16.

3.127 August-born children often enter reception class immediately after their fourth birthday while September-born children are more likely to do so immediately before their fifth birthday. August-born children will be three months away from their eleventh birthday when they take Key Stage 2 tests, September-born children will be only four months away from their twelfth. Although the gap in attainment does reduce over time, it still has a significant impact on whether young people go on to higher education.

3.128 Many of the measures already outlined in this chapter will have a positive impact on summer-born children – smoothing transitions into and between schools, reforming the primary curriculum, personalising learning and shifting to single level tests taken when ready. We will also work to raise awareness of teachers and school leaders about this issue.

3.129 In addition, we believe there is a case for examining whether changes in the arrangements for entry to primary school could help summer-born children. Research evidence suggests that allowing all children in a year group to begin at the same time (the September of the year they turn 5) has the most positive impact as it allows summer-born children to receive the same amount of full-time schooling as their peers.

3.130 However, we know that some parents have concerns about the readiness of their summer-born children to join primary school. As part of his work on the Review of the Primary Curriculum, the details of which are set out above, we will ask Sir Jim Rose to consider how we can design the curriculum to improve outcomes for summer-born children and whether it would be appropriate to allow greater flexibility in start dates.

Gifted and talented

3.131 Starting with the first Excellence in Cities programme in 1999, we have built a strong national programme for gifted and talented pupils in schools. We want to ensure that all schools and colleges identify and support a representative population of gifted and talented learners. Already 91 per cent of secondary schools and 65 per cent of primary schools have identified some 733,000 learners. Once all schools and colleges are involved, by 2010, the national programme will be supporting about one million learners.

3.132 All gifted and talented learners aged 4–19 are eligible for support provided through Young Gifted and Talented, who are developing a 'one-stop shop' approach to support for gifted and talented learners, their parents and teachers. Every school has access to a leading teacher for gifted and talented education and to an extensive national training and support programme.

3.133 To increase schools' focus on the achievements of gifted and talented learners, **we plan to publish new indicators to show the peformance of pupils achieving Level 7 or above in English, mathematics and science and achieving Level 8 and above in mathematics, to ensure proper attention is given to gifted and talented learners**. From February 2008 personalisation will help ensure that gifted and talented children all make at least two levels of progress in each Key Stage, especially disadvantaged learners more likely to be underachieving. Through City Challenge we are now seeking to help gifted and talented learners by:

- raising pupils', parents' and communities' aspirations so students from poor backgrounds seek to enter the most competitive higher education institutions and courses;

- providing a coherent support programme across Years 10–13 so the most disadvantaged gifted and talented learners can achieve good qualifications; and

- improving the identification of disadvantaged gifted and talented learners.

Conclusion

3.134 This chapter set out our plans for giving each child the best start in life through quality early years childcare and early learning, built upon by personalised teaching and learning in school that addresses each child's individual needs. In each area, this chapter also sets out the steps that we will take. In addition, we will revise the Delivery Agreement for our Public Service Agreements on raising the educational achievement of all children and young people (PSA 10) and on narrowing the gap in educational achievement between children from low income and disadvantaged backgrounds and their peers (PSA11) so that they reflect the Children's Plan.

3.135 Chapter 4 sets out how we will deliver this vision of personalised children's services across early years settings and schools.

Chapter 4: Leadership and collaboration

System reform to achieve world class standards and close the gap in educational achievement for children from disadvantaged families

Executive summary

4.1 If we are to achieve the potential improvement in standards from personalisation, we need to create an early years and schools system where all institutions are consistently achieving at the level of the best.

4.2 The single most important factor in delivering our aspirations for children is a world class workforce able to provide highly personalised support so we will continue to drive up quality and capacity of those working in the children's workforce. We know from our consultation how important the quality of early years childcare and education is to improving children's achievement. So we will invest £117 million over the next three years in the early years workforce, including measures to:

- fund supply cover so early years workers can take part in continuous professional development; and

- boost the graduate leader fund so that every full daycare setting will be led by a graduate by 2015, with two graduates per setting in disadvantaged areas.

4.3 We already have many teachers and headteachers who are among the best in the world. However, to deliver a teaching workforce and a new generation of headteachers which is consistently world class we will allocate £44 million over the next three years to:

- make teaching a Masters level profession by working with the social partnership to introduce a new qualification, building on the recently agreed performance management measures;

- ensure new recruits spend at least one year in training;

- establish a Transition to Teaching programme to attract more people with science, technology and engineering backgrounds into teaching; and

- extend the Future Leaders programme which places people with proven leadership credentials into urban schools.

4.4 By promoting diversity in a collaborative system we can ensure that children, young people and parents are able to choose provision that reflects their particular needs. Schools and other settings can use their increased freedoms to innovate and find new solutions to problems, which can then be shared with others to ensure all children benefit. To strengthen both diversity and collaboration, we are expecting every secondary school to have specialist, trust or academy status and every school to have a business or university partner, with 230 academies by 2010 on the road to 400. Through strengthened accountability and governance, we will build on the successes of the last ten years in reducing the number of failing schools. We expect local authorities to take swift and decisive action to prevent schools from failing and to reverse failure quickly when it happens. We also expect local authorities actively to challenge schools who are not improving their pupils' performance but are coasting. We have already set a goal that within five years no secondary school should have fewer than 30 per cent of pupils gaining 5 higher level GCSEs. To improve the quality of accountability and governance and in addition to our measures to strengthen parental engagement in schools we will:

- make governing bodies more effective, beginning by consulting on reducing the size of governing bodies.

Chapter 7 sets out further detail on how we expect schools to work together and with other services to break down barriers to learning.

4.5   We know that standards of behaviour continue to be a matter of concern for parents, teachers, and children and young people themselves. It is important that the environment in every classroom supports effective teaching and learning and we have made it easier for teachers to enforce discipline and good behaviour. We currently expect secondary schools to be in behaviour partnerships, as recommended in Sir Alan Steer's 2005 report, to work together to improve behaviour and tackle persistent absence as well as improve outcomes for those whose behaviour is poor. Sir Alan's report recommended that participation in behaviour partnerships should be compulsory from 2008. Given that 97 per cent of schools are already participating, we are minded to implement this recommendation and will:

- ask Sir Alan Steer to review progress since his report and the effectiveness of behaviour partnerships; and

- depending on his findings make participation in them compulsory for all maintained schools and all new academies, encouraging all existing academies to take part as well.

4.6   Children who behave poorly and are excluded, those unable to attend a mainstream school and those disengaged from education are a relatively small proportion of pupils. However, they include some of the young people with the worst prospects for success in later life, and most likely to develop problem behaviours. The quality of education they receive is highly variable despite the difference it can make to their prospects. To address this we will:

- spend £26.5 million over the next three years on piloting new forms of alternative provision which could include using small schools – studio schools – with close links to business and providing a high quality vocational education; and

- ask local authorities to collect and publish performance data for pupils not on a school roll, to ensure local areas have incentives to improve their performance.

4.7   To deliver world class education and children's services we need world class buildings and use of technology. We will continue with our unprecedented investment in the fabric of schools and children and young people's services to create schools fit for the 21st century and will:

- produce guidance to ensure that where possible new buildings make space for co-located services; and

- set an ambition for all new school buildings to be zero carbon by 2016. We know that with the technologies currently available, the zero carbon ambition cannot be achieved on many school sites. We are therefore appointing a taskforce to advise on how to achieve zero carbon schools, whether the timescale is realistic and how to reduce carbon emissions in the intervening period.

Key areas for reform

4.8 Building on the progress the Government has already achieved in driving up standards and quality of provision for children and young people and on the unprecedented investment in children's services, we are taking action in four key areas:

- **world class early years and schools workforce:** we will improve the quality of frontline practitioners in early years settings as well as schools, and support leaders and managers;

- **diversity and collaboration for success:** we will continue to develop a diverse system in which institutions work together, learn from each other and thereby drive up quality across the board;

- **accountability and governance to drive improvement:** we will support a system in which the local authority, inspectorates and parents play their part in improving quality and standards; and

- **the right conditions for teaching and learning:** we will take tough action on poor standards of behaviour, provide better alternative education so that excluded pupils do not continue to fail and will ensure that the buildings in which children learn are suited to 21st century needs.

World class early years and schools workforce

Recruitment and retention in the early years workforce

4.9 We know that high quality early years education, alongside the home learning environment, can give children a head start when they enter school and that this is sustained until at least age 10. This is why we have a Public Service Agreement to raise attainment and close the gap in the Early Years Foundation Stage (EYFS). Getting the best out of early years provision depends on the quality of the workforce and the quality of leadership of the settings or schools. This was highlighted by the 0–7 Expert Group.

4.10 The early years sector is highly diverse, with 80 per cent of provision from private, voluntary and independent (PVI) providers. We have regulated to set the core standards we expect every early years provider and childminder to achieve, and these standards are set out in the Early Years Foundation Stage (EYFS).

4.11 However, despite rapid growth in the number of better trained practitioners there remains a skill and qualifications gap between the workforce in the maintained sector and that in PVI settings and childminders. Public funding and demand from parents need to create a higher quality early years workforce.

4.12 The Government is allocating significant levels of funding to improve the quality of provision in the early years. Over £400 million is being made available between 2008 and 2011 for quality improvement. This includes funding for Level 3 qualifications and the £175 million Graduate Leader Fund, designed to secure a cadre of graduate-level professionals leading practice in PVI full daycare settings.

4.13 **We will boost the graduate leader fund so that every full day care setting will be led by a graduate by 2015, with two graduates per setting in disadvantaged areas.**

Recruitment and retention of excellent school teachers

4.14 Improving teacher quality is the single biggest driver for improving educational standards, and we already have many teachers who compare with the best in the world. Teaching is the profession of choice for many top graduates, and we want it to attract even more of the brightest and the best applicants. If we want to have a world class education system, we must also continue to focus on all teachers developing their professional skills to the highest level.

4.15 Over the next three years, we will be recruiting more than 100,000 people to train as teachers. The quality of entrants to teaching has improved over the last decade and we are also recruiting a growing number of people changing careers, who bring a different set of skills into the classroom, and in many cases add valuable managerial and leadership skills. 30 per cent of all first year teacher trainees are now aged 30 or over, compared with 26 per cent in 1998/99, and so are likely to be career changers.

4.16 To improve further the quality of the teaching workforce, we want to attract a bigger pool of high quality applicants to teacher training. Alongside the most popular route – the post-graduate certificate in education, or PGCE – we now offer undergraduate courses, 'on-the-job' training such as the Graduate Teacher Programme, and Teach First, which has now expanded from London to Manchester and the Midlands and is due to expand further.

4.17 We safeguard entry to the profession with the award of Qualified Teacher Status (QTS). While Ofsted has noted that we now have the best new recruits ever into the profession, it has also observed that not all routes into teaching have been delivering equally high standards. And so, **from 2008, we will ensure that new recruits spend at least one year in training Graduate Teacher Programme**. In circumstances where recruits have a high level of experience, they may be able to qualify earlier.

Box 4.1: Teaching as a high status profession

The Children's Plan is designed to help teachers and school leaders enable every child and young person to fulfil their potential, and to make teaching an even higher status profession. Over the past four years Government has worked closely with its social partners, and they have made a huge contribution to the improvements that have been made for children and families. We are committed to ensuring that teachers' workload is manageable, to tackling long hours and ensuring they benefit from existing statutory provisions. It is crucial the to success of the Children's Plan that we continue remodelling the school workforce, so that teachers can concentrate on teaching as well as being able to draw effectively on wider children's services to support them.

Mathematics and science

4.18 We have set ourselves tough targets to make sure there are enough specialist mathematics and science teachers to teach young people to be able to progress into careers which demand these sought-after skills.

4.19 We pay the highest level of teacher training bursary and 'golden hello' for mathematics and science, and additional payments are made to initial teacher training providers for each mathematics, physics or chemistry trainee teacher they recruit. We are funding professional development for science educators, and are keen that schools should improve their use of existing pay flexibilities for recruitment and retention.

4.20 **We will establish a Transition to Teaching programme to attract more people with science, technology and engineering backgrounds into teaching.** This is an industry-led programme to encourage suitable people with a background in science, technology, engineering or mathematics (STEM) into teaching. Making use of the skills they bring from their careers will help bring these subjects alive . Larry Hirst, the Chief Executive of IBM UK, is leading the Steering Group guiding the development of Transition to Teaching, with the aim of increasing the number of teachers with both subject expertise and the experience of applying that knowledge.

Continuing professional development

4.21 Everyone working in early years, schools and colleges should be committed to continuing professional development (CPD), to learn from best practice and to keep their skills up to date. This is particularly important as we move to an increasingly personalised approach to teaching and learning as set out in Chapter 3, and to support integrated working with other professionals. This plan thus sets out new entitlements and expectations for the workforce.

> *"We need workers involved with children and families who are both linked into communities but who are also well trained and skilled."*
> *(Respondent to Online Survey working with children and young people)*

Early years

4.22 To gain the benefits of early years education, practitioners need to be working at the cutting edge of practice. We want to see early years practitioners and teachers securing core qualifications and continuously updating their skills and knowledge. To support this, we will put in place an expanded programme of CPD – delivered by National Strategies – focused on supporting key aspects of children's learning and development as well as on narrowing gaps in outcomes between disadvantaged children and their peers.

4.23 We recognise that it can be difficult for settings, particularly in the PVI sector, to accommodate day release for practitioners. **We will fund supply cover so early years workers can take part in continuing professional development.**

Schools

4.24 Teaching is a highly skilled, high status occupation. The best teachers constantly seek to improve and develop their skills and subject knowledge. **To help fulfil our high ambitions for all children, and to boost the status of teaching still further, we now want it to become a masters-level profession. We will make teaching a masters level profession by working with the social partnership to introduce a new qualification, building on the recently agreed performance management measures.** To ensure the best possible quality of teaching in all schools, we have already taken steps to ensure that every teacher will now be engaged in high quality performance management linked to continued practical professional development from when they first start teaching. Our new goal will be for all teachers to achieve a Masters qualification as a result over the course of their career. This will represent a step change for the profession that will bring us in line with the highest performing education systems in the world. We will work within the social partnership for school workforce reform and with the Training and Development Agency for Schools (TDA) to agree how we realise our ambitions in this area.

4.25 All new recruits should thus benefit from a more structured approach to their early professional development. This will help them to develop more effectively the classroom skills they need such as assessment for learning and recognising and responding to children and families with special needs. We will work with the TDA to ensure that all teachers have the opportunity to engage in collaborative CPD that focuses on classroom practice. We will encourage new forms of professional development where groups of teachers meet frequently to evaluate and improve their teaching.

4.26 To meet our ambitious 2020 goals, we will need to bring all teachers up to the quality of those who are already excellent in their subjects. We will continue to invest in a national programme to support high quality teaching in English and mathematics, provided through the Primary and Secondary National Strategies, as set out in Chapter 3.

4.27 We will keep the new performance management arrangements for teachers under review while we explore with social partners how to frame a contractual entitlement to CPD so that it best supports teachers' professional development.

4.28 Finally, to be sure that parents and pupils can continue to have confidence in the skills of the workforce, we will look with social partners at whether more can be done to address the performance of teachers who have the greatest difficulty in carrying out their role effectively. This should include helping them to leave the profession if that is appropriate. We will also work with the General Teaching Council to examine whether action is needed to ensure that in the rare cases where competence falls to unacceptably low levels their QTS status is withdrawn, meaning that they are no longer permitted to teach as a qualified teacher in a maintained school.

Support staff

4.29   Schools employ an increasingly diverse workforce. There are now double the number of support staff in schools since 1997, with over 308,000 full-time equivalent support staff working in schools. Almost 164,000 of these are teaching assistants. In keeping with the National Agreement on Raising Standards and Tackling Workload – signed in January 2003 by the Government, local government employers and the vast majority of school workforce unions – new roles have been created, such as higher level teaching assistants, School Business Managers, cover supervisors and exams officers.

4.30   This new workforce has made a huge difference to teaching and learning. It has freed up teacher time, allowing them to concentrate on the classroom. It strengthens the personalised support individual children can be given through small group and one-to-one provision.

4.31   We want to ensure that all schools fully exploit the potential of this workforce. In 2006, the TDA published a three-year plan Developing people to support learning: a skills strategy for the wider school workforce 2006–09. **We will ask TDA to work with the National College for School Leadership (NCSL) to refresh this strategy to ensure that it is properly aligned with the vision of the 21st century school** set out in the Children's Plan, and takes proper account of the increasingly diverse range of support staff in our schools.

4.32   We have also made a commitment to ensure that support staff are fairly rewarded for the work they do. A new negotiating council will be established to develop a bespoke framework that will present a nationally consistent approach to support staff employment matters whilst containing sufficient flexibility to help meet local needs. The framework will be used by school governing bodies and local authorities to determine pay and conditions for support staff employed in all maintained schools in England. These arrangements will ensure that heads have greater clarity and that support staff themselves benefit from a more appropriate, tailored and transparent set of arrangements.

Leadership

4.33   Delivering a world class system will rely upon confident leaders who can deliver excellence in their own institutions and can work with other leaders to provide the best possible services for children and young people.

Leading the early years sector

4.34   Leaders in the early years sector need to set a clear vision for quality and improvement in settings and lead a positive learning culture in which all staff continually reflect on and improve their practice. They also need to be committed to learning from the best. Leaders in a world class early years sector will be instrumental in embedding continuous quality improvement in settings – thus focusing on the needs of every individual child – but also in helping to shape and raise parents' expectations of the quality they can expect from early learning.

4.35   The Children's Workforce Development Council (CWDC) is already establishing networks that will allow newly qualified early years professionals (including qualified teachers) to exchange experience and best practice. We will develop as part of our proposals for partnership, networking and professional development a new focus on early years leadership, focusing on the change management and leadership skills required to deliver a continuously improving service in a mixed market. This work will be led by the Primary National Strategies and will begin by supporting leaders and managers in disadvantaged areas.

4.36 Sharing knowledge, expertise and data across schools and early years settings is vital to support children's successful transition from early learning. This will improve children's outcomes and wellbeing and their achievement once they start school. Many schools already have close links with early years settings in their local area, but the picture is by no means uniform. **The Government will therefore spend £15 million over three years to promote buddying and other joint work between schools and early years settings**. Building on current work undertaken by the CWDC, an early years professional or graduate leader will have the opportunity to work shadow or take up joint training with primary school teachers.

4.37 We have established national standards for Sure Start Children's Centre leaders and over 700 managers have already taken the National Professional Qualification in Integrated Centre Leadership. We will continue to encourage all centre managers to take this qualification.

School leadership

4.38 Success in our programmes for children and young people depends on having great leaders in our schools. Over 60 per cent of heads are now over 50, which means over the next decade a whole generation of school leaders will be retiring. Dealing with the loss of their skills and experience will be a challenge, but this is also an opportunity for innovation and reform. The National College for School Leadership's succession planning strategy is aimed at recruiting a new generation of leaders to head our schools in the next 20 years.

4.39 These leaders will need to have the support and the breadth of skills and knowledge necessary to run the 21st century school, providing an excellent education, delivering extended services and playing a role in supporting all aspects of children's lives. This was also highlighted by the 8–13 Expert Group. **A redesigned qualification for headship, the revised National Professional Qualification for Headship, will start in 2008** designed with these wider responsibilities in mind. This will be aligned with the National Professional Qualification for Integrated Centre Leadership programme for children's centre managers (see above).

4.40 We also recognise that leaders of 21st century schools face increasingly complex management challenges and schools do not always have the right mix of skills to tackle them. To address these challenges, we have asked the NCSL to run 24 demonstration projects testing the new roles of Advanced School Business Manager and of School Business Director. These roles are designed to give headteachers the space to focus on teaching and learning and improving performance.

4.41 Remodelling the leadership team is about new skills but also developing existing skills and spotting and nurturing talent. We are therefore working with social partners to review the professional responsibilities of all teachers, including headteachers, and developing new standards for school leadership. The NCSL is also investigating models of leadership that reflect the role of a modern school leader.

4.42 The National Leaders of Education and National Support Schools Programme are helping schools in special measures – with evidence of success. **We will do more for challenging schools by extending the National Leaders of Education programme in both secondary and primary schools.** We will seek to create a pool of high quality experienced heads ready to take on challenging schools including complex schools in our most deprived areas.

Box 4.2: School leaders transforming schools

Debden Park, Essex and Kemnal Technology College, Kent

Debden Park, an 11–16 school of 870 pupils which moved into new accommodation in 2001, was placed in special measures in January 2007. It was graded 4 (inadequate), for all aspects of performance. John Atkins, the Head of Kemnal Technology College in Bromley who is a National Leader in Education, took over as Executive Head of Debden. This has led to a remarkable turnaround in a very short time. The school had its second monitoring inspection recently and was not only removed from special measures but given an Ofsted grade 2 (good). The average turnaround time for a secondary school in special measures is now 22 months and at 9 months Debden's turnaround time is one of the fastest and most effective.

Greenwood Dale School and River Leen School, Nottingham

Since November 2006 Barry Day, headteacher at Greenwood Dale School in Nottingham, has been working closely with the acting headteacher at River Leen School. This work has included his deputy and senior staff setting up a joint project team with staff from River Leen to address student underperformance. The work has also involved one of his assistant heads taking responsibility for specifically improving the teaching of mathematics, and ensuring that the Year 11 students have benefited from more personalised learning. The partnership between the two schools has brought some excellent results. 41 per cent of Year 11 students at River Leen achieved five or more A*–C grades in 2007, compared to only 23 per cent in 2006. 14 per cent gained five or more A*–C grade, including mathematics and English, up from 4 per cent in 2006. Barry Day commented that "these improved results show just how effective partnership working can be. Staff from both schools have worked hard together for the benefit of students at the school. Greenwood Dale results have risen again this year, despite our work in other schools. Over 80 per cent of students at Greenwood Dale gained five or more A*–C grades, up from 78 per cent in 2006".

Joseph Ruston Technology College and the Priory LSST, Lincolnshire

In autumn 2005, Joseph Ruston Technology College was on the brink of failure, with only 17 per per cent of pupils gaining five or more GCSEs at grade C or better. Richard Gilliland, the head of the highly successful Priory LSST School then took over as Executive Head teacher, and has forged a revolution in standards and ethos at Joseph Ruston. In 2006, the proportion of pupils with five or more GCSEs at grade C or better rose to 39 per cent and this year's provisional results are an excellent 71 per cent. Although there is still scope for improvements in English and mathematics, the school's science results have risen substantially since 2005. Pupils' behaviour, and the culture for learning within the school, have been transformed. These improvements will be sustained through plans to make both Joseph Ruston Technology College and the Priory LSST School part of a three school academy trust under Richard Gilliland's leadership.

Getting the best teachers and leaders into disadvantaged areas

4.43　We have targeted programmes to improve the quality of leadership for disadvantaged children who need it most, such as Teach First. In its succession planning strategy to bring on the next generation of school leaders, the NCSL will test **additional targeted support to 40 local authorities which have the highest risk of hard-to-fill headship vacancies**.

4.44　We need to continue to attract an increasingly diverse mix of people into school leadership. The Future Leaders programme is already piloting a radically new approach to the development of urban school leaders by bringing people with proven leadership credentials and without teaching experience into the workforce. **We will extend the Future Lenders programme which places people with proven leadership credentials into urban schools** so that, by September 2011, there will be over 500 Future Leaders in schools across the country's major city regions, working together to improve outcomes for children and lead system change.

Integrated working in a preventative system

4.45　In the preventative system the Children's Plan has set out as its vision, everyone working in a school or an early years setting – teachers, early years practitioners, leaders and support staff – will need to have the necessary skills to work with other services and professionals to provide the additional support that some children will need. This will strengthen their ability to tackle barriers to learning that cannot be overcome in the classroom. Teachers and early years practitioners, who come into very regular contact with children, will not be expected to work outside their competence, but we will want to ensure they are all able systematically to spot potential problems early and refer them on to in-house or other support. The NCSL will support all levels of school leaders in the further development of the Every Child Matters approach – by embedding this into all programmes. Chapter 7 describes our wider vision for integrated working across the whole children's workforce.

4.46　For school staff and early years practitioners CPD will also be important for gaining the specialist skills that they require to better meet the wide-ranging challenges that they face on a daily basis:

- transitions into school from the early years;
- the need to engage all parents as partners in their children's learning and development;
- additional needs and SEN, in particular so that these needs can be identified early and the appropriate referrals can be made to specialist support;
- the need for interagency working and collaboration including access to the whole range of children's services; and
- challenging behaviour in the classroom or setting.

Box 4.3: The school workforce offer – summary

The quality of the school workforce is critical to meeting our ambitions. To support the school workforce the Children's Plan sets out the following commitments:

- stipulating the minimum time student teachers must spend in training when on a one-year Graduate Teacher Programme;

- developing Transition to Teaching to attract more science, mathematics and ICT teachers;

- developing a more structured approach to teachers' early professional development;

- setting out an ambition that teaching should become increasingly a Masters-level profession;

- continued investment in a national programme to support high quality teaching in English and mathematics, through the Primary and Secondary National strategies;

- refreshing the skills strategy for the wider schools workforce;

- fair rewards for support staff through the creation of a new negotiating council to develop a framework for their pay and conditions;

- redesign of the National Professional Qualification for Headship;

- launch of projects to test the roles of Advanced School Business Manager and School Business Director;

- extension of the National Leaders of Education programme

- targeted support from NCSL to local authorities which have the highest risk of hard-to-fill headship vacancies; and

- the extension of the Future Leaders programme.

Diversity and collaboration for success

4.47 Over the last ten years, we have promoted diversity of provision throughout 0–19 learning. We have done this to provide choices so that the needs of children, young people and their families can be met; to give providers freedom to innovate; and to create healthy competition between providers as an incentive to respond to local demand.

4.48 This has brought huge benefits. In the early years sector, we now have a range of providers able to offer flexible quality provision that helps parents to balance work and home life. Specialist schools and academies are popular with parents and deliver better results, in particular for disadvantaged children.

4.49 However, to capture the full benefits of a diverse system, providers also need to work collaboratively, because we want all children to benefit from innovation and best practice. The evidence shows that clusters, collaborative partnerships and federations between providers can bring huge benefits, in terms of pooling expertise, generating efficiencies to allow more to be spent on teaching and learning, smoothing transitions between phases, and sharing successful leaders with weaker schools. Collaborative working also helps to provide more and better specialist provision, for example in welfare services, provision for excluded pupils and many other areas. We support collaborative working between education providers as well as between schools and early years settings and other services such as health and the voluntary and community sector, as set out in Chapter 7.

Early years quality through 0–7 partnerships

4.50 Sharing of expertise between schools, Sure Start Children's Centres, early years and childcare providers and the health service helps improve the lives of young people and their families – by creating a higher quality, more seamless service designed around their needs. We therefore **propose to invest £10 million over three years to identify best practice and test new partnership models at locality level, piloting 0–7 partnerships in a small number of areas**. 0–7 partnerships will operate within the Children's Trust and promote continuity for children and families from birth through to age 7. They will support stronger engagement with parents, which was identified as a key issue by the 0–7 Expert Group. We will work with a range of stakeholders to develop the pilots.

School diversity

4.51 The number of self-governing schools is increasing. We now have 83 academies – with 133 expected to be open by September 2008. The first 30 schools became trust schools in September 2007, and with around 170 are in the pipeline. In addition, there are 2,800 specialist secondary schools providing particular subject expertise. Greater diversity in the school system is enhancing the quality of education provision and in turn improving the choice of good school places for children and parents, especially where education providers are building partnerships with each other and with businesses, further and higher education institutions and the voluntary sector.

4.52 We want to see **every secondary school working towards specialist, academy or trust status** so that all children enjoy the benefits this can bring. We also expect increasing numbers of schools to work closely with partners. Indeed, we want every secondary school to have a university or business partner. And because academies can bring particular benefits to disadvantaged areas by injecting fresh ideas and leadership where all else has failed, we are committed to at least 230 academies by 2010.

Box 4.4: Diversity in the school system

Specialist schools are maintained secondary schools which have chosen to focus on one of ten curriculum areas as a driver to raise whole-school standards. Over 86 per cent of secondary schools are now specialist. Specialist school status is linked to high results at GCSE, whether this is on the five or more A*–C measure, Value Added (VA) or Contextual Value Added (CVA). We ask specialist schools to use at least a third of their funding to disseminate good practice in their curriculum area, for example, through making specialist facilities and teaching available to other schools. Collaboration between schools with different specialisms and their links with the community and businesses increases the range of experiences on offer to pupils.

Academies are all-ability state-funded schools established and managed by independent sponsors. Academies are set up where the local status quo in secondary education is simply not good enough and where there is demand for new high quality school places. Sponsors challenge traditional thinking on how schools are run and what they should be like for students. This helps to raise standards and foster innovation and best practice, which can then benefit other schools. Each academy has an endowment, the proceeds of which are channelled back to the local community.

Trust schools are maintained foundation schools supported by a charitable trust, enabling schools to forge long-term sustainable relationships with external partners from further and higher education, business, and the voluntary sector, to create a new source of dynamism and to help raise standards. Working with other schools, trusts are sharing teaching and learning across schools to deliver for example the 14–19 offer and extended services. The first 30 trust schools opened in September 2007. We are currently well on track to achieving our aspirational target of having 300 schools becoming or working towards trust school status by the end of 2008.

4.53 A range of provision is needed in both mainstream and special schools to meet the diverse needs of children with SEN and disabilities. Special schools play an important role in meeting the needs of children with severe and complex difficulties, working with mainstream schools. Capacity in the mainstream school system to meet the needs of children with special educational needs is developed by collaboration between schools and outreach work by special schools.

School collaboration and federation

4.54 Building on evidence about the benefits of collaboration and school improvement partnerships, we want to facilitate greater opportunities for federations between primaries and a single secondary. This has been shown to bring benefits – as the 8–13 Expert Group recognised. It could allow sharing of specialisms and equipment, and smooth transitions between primary and secondary, where the evidence shows performance often drops as children adjust to a new, larger setting. It would increase opportunities to stretch the most able pupils in primary schools and provide easier access to Gifted and Talented provision. It can also help schools to develop extended services.

4.55 We know collaboration works, and we strongly encourage schools to build on informal partnerships through federations. Federations with a single governing body and pooled budgets can bring about real efficiency gains through shared services and facilities and increased CPD opportunities for staff. Strong schools have a particular role to play here, using federations with weaker schools to drive up standards and disseminate best practice, enabling more schools to benefit from the very best leadership available.

4.56 Trust status provides an opportunity for schools to collaborate, underpinned by the added expertise, support, drive and ethos of partners from the voluntary, business, higher and further education sectors. It enables schools to benefit from the fresh insight and problem solving skills of their partners.

4.57 Many of the early Trust School Pathfinders focused particularly on collaborating to extend opportunity for 14–19-year-olds. At secondary level, it is increasingly important that schools work with each other and with colleges and other providers. By 2013, all 14–19-year-olds will have a new entitlement to curriculum and qualifications – including an entitlement to study whichever of the new Diplomas they choose at whatever level is appropriate to them, as set out in Chapter 5. This new entitlement goes beyond what any one school could offer alone, and requires consortia of schools and colleges to work together in new ways. Many such consortia are already working together across the country to make this successful, developing common curriculum frameworks, processes and accountability arrangements, which are proving successful in giving more young people access to learning opportunities which engage and excite them and enable them to achieve.

4.58 Chapters 5 and 7 set out in detail the collaboration needed between schools, and between schools and other partners, necessary to provide the full range of services and educational options children, young people and families need and want.

Box 4.5: Ashington Trust

In Ashington, Northumberland, five of the largest schools in the town have joined in partnership to form a trust. The trust will facilitate greater and more effective collaboration in education provision for 3,000 pupils aged 3–19. It will also see the linking of four of the schools, Wansbeck First School, Bothal and Hirst Park Middle Schools and Ashington High School Sports College in a hard federation. Kenneth Tonge, currently Head of Ashington High School Sports College, has been appointed as strategic head of the trust and will take up his new post on 1 January 2008.

The aim of the trust is to equip children and young people with the skills they need through a more coherent all age education. The trust will work with a range of partners: Northumberland Local Authority, the University of Northumbria, Northumberland College, the Wansbeck Business Forum, and Ashington NCH Children's Centre. This is to encourage better opportunities for lifelong learning, better student preparation for employment and ongoing education, improved community involvement, better facilities and extended support for families. Together with its partners the trust also wants to establish a coherent learning pathway from early years through to further and higher education.

Mobilisation of support for education

4.59 We want the whole of society to support learning and development – encouraging all sectors, not least business and academia, to help raise the aspirations of children, young people and their parents, and to work with early years providers, schools and colleges directly to raise standards. The National Council for Educational Excellence has a very important role as advocate and champion to rally businesses and universities to support educational excellence as well as to promote partnerships between early years providers, schools and colleges.

Fair admissions

4.60 The full benefits of school diversity must be made available to every child if we are to reach our ambitious goals. We need fair admissions systems, giving every child an equal opportunity to go to a school of their parents' choice, regardless of their personal circumstances or background.

4.61 The School Admissions Code came into force in February 2007 and all schools and local authorities are required to comply with it. The Code prohibits a range of unfair and subjective admissions criteria and practices. The Government will measure and monitor its impact on children and families over time. The Code requires each area to agree to make sure that children arriving in an area outside the normal time of admission are offered places quickly and that the most vulnerable children (including excluded children and those with challenging behaviour) are placed in the most suitable school rather the one that simply has places available. Children in care now also have the highest priority in school admissions arrangements; and we have extended rights to free school transport for low income families. We have provided guidelines to ensure other school policies, such as on uniforms and school trips, do not discriminate against disadvantaged families or discourage applications from certain groups.

4.62 Clear and straightforward information on admissions is essential if parents are to make informed school choices. Choice advisers are now operating in 126 local authorities (as at the end of November 2007) and we expect them to be available in all authorities by September 2008, offering parents, especially disadvantaged parents, support with secondary school applications. Parents also now have the right to object to the Schools Adjudicator about any unlawful admissions arrangements in schools in their area and are increasingly using this new power. To further strengthen support for parents, we will consult on improvements to the school application and allocation process to make it easier for parents to use.

Accountability and governance to drive improvement

4.63 Diversity of provision, collaboration and fair admissions will all help drive school improvement. But to make sure that children and young people are not let down by failing institutions, and receive a high quality education, we need to ensure the right accountability, governance and improvement strategies are in place.

4.64 Parents have a vital role to play in improving provision, as set out in Chapter 3. Equally, local authorities are critical to the delivery of improvements across all children's services – this was also recognised by all three Expert Groups in their reports. As set out in the Introduction, we expect local authorities and all the partners on the Children's Trust to champion and take responsibility for achieving measurable improvements in outcomes for children across all five of the Every Child Matters outcomes.

Improving early years provision

4.65 Improving early years settings requires not just committed leaders and managers but also a strong role for local authorities in managing the local early years market to deliver improvement. Local authorities need a clear strategy for improving the skills and capability of the early years workforce to ensure that they meet the standards of the Early Years Foundation Stage. The National Strategies will provide challenge and support to local authorities on their early years work. They will focus on identifying and promoting effective practice and on the use of data to monitor and track children's developmental progress and identify where additional support is needed.

4.66 The Childcare Act 2006 places a legal duty on local authorities to improve outcomes for all young children and allows for statutory targets for children's outcomes at age 5. Feedback from the first round of setting these targets suggests that they are already making higher standards in the early years a priority for local authorities.

4.67 In addition, Ofsted will introduce a new framework from September 2008 alongside the Early Years Foundation Stage. The new framework will bring together inspection of early learning and care, providing genuinely comparable judgements across all Sure Start Children's Centres, schools, and PVI settings offering early years provision. Ofsted will inspect whether children are safe and whether the quality of their care is improved.

4.68 The Government will set out what high quality early years provision looks like and will maintain and extend core financial support for the workforce, focused on graduate leadership and progression. We will monitor progress in improving the quality of the workforce through the annual Early Years and Childcare Providers Survey and through the work of the CWDC – informing local authority work to improve early years provision.

School improvement

4.69 The number of failing schools and those with unacceptably low attainment has reduced substantially in the last decade. The number of schools with under one quarter of pupils gaining five GCSEs at grade A*–C has fallen from 616 in 1997 to only 26 today – a 24-fold reduction. This means fewer children are being failed by a poor education in a weak institution.

4.70 We have now set ourselves the goal that within five years no secondary school should have fewer than 30 per cent of pupils gaining five GCSEs at grade A*–C including English and mathematics. In 1997 over half of schools were below this threshold, now under a quarter are, but the waste of talent and potential this represents is not acceptable. Many of these schools are already improving rapidly and we are expecting them to lift their own performance above the threshold.

4.71 However, lifting all schools above a floor will not create a world class education system. We must now rise to the challenge of creating a consistently excellent system, where all schools are reaching the level of the best. We will achieve this through a local accountability system focused on promoting continuing improvement in the classroom, and in which we act decisively to:

- **eradicate failure**, addressing the underperformance that is often a prelude to failure, and not tolerate failure where it occurs;

- **challenge complacency** and in doing so work to **eliminate wide variations within a school** – where average whole-school performance masks some very poor standards in some areas; and

- **incentivise every school to improve** – driving satisfactory and good schools to become outstanding organisations and promoting a culture of ambition across the sector.

4.72 We set out further steps we will take to achieve a more consistently excellent system below. Excellence relies on the expertise of our national partners, and we will discuss with our partners how to provide incentives for competent and good schools that have the potential to become outstanding, world class providers and then sustain increased levels of success.

Governing bodies

4.73 Governing bodies challenge and support schools to set a strong vision and to provide the best service they can for the children and parents in their communities. This is a demanding role and governors need support and development to play it – but needs will differ and so we will **review our training programme for governors to ensure it supports new ways of working in a smaller, strategically focused governing body**. As part of this we will be working with the NCSL and other partners to develop new training for new chairs of governors.

4.74 Smaller governing bodies tend to be more effective and highly skilled. We believe smaller governing bodies can be consistent with the stakeholder model and **so we will make governing bodies more effective, beginning by consulting on reducing the size of governing bodies**.

Inspection

4.75 There has been significant reform to school inspection in recent years. Inspections are now shorter and sharper, based on data as well as on the school's own assessment of its performance and areas for improvement. Inspection judgements focus on a school's understanding of its overall effectiveness and its capacity to identify and act to improve these areas. More complacent and less dynamic schools in the system are inspected more frequently and in more depth than stronger schools.

4.76 The Ofsted inspection framework will be reviewed in September 2009, coinciding with a new inspection cycle that will place more emphasis on inspection according to risk. **As outlined in Chapter 7, we will develop strong indicators for all the Every Child Matters outcomes at school level**, to ensure that schools are being measured and rewarded for their contribution to children's wellbeing as well as to educational attainment and progress.

Local authorities

4.77 Local government is uniquely placed to improve outcomes for all children and young people. It holds a democratic mandate to act in the interests of local people – including children – and respond to their need and concerns. As part of this, local authorities need to play a central role in securing improvements of both failing and coasting schools. They have been given clear responsibility for improving children's services, working with local health and other partners and the voluntary and community sector to make sure that every child gets the best possible start in life, putting the best interests of children, young people and parents first, whether they are acting as commissioner or direct provider of services.

4.78 The role of local authorities in education has changed, from provider to strategic commissioner. This role demands that local authorities:

- *develop strong sustainable relationships* both in the community they serve, and among the providers who are best placed to deliver an effective and joined up service to children and young people and their families;

- *commission* services around the child, whether school places, extended school services, or targeted support like CAMHS, SEN, or specialist social services assistance;

- *intervene* in any service, whether provided by a school, a local agency or partner, or indeed by the authority itself, where services are not being delivered effectively; and

- where appropriate, *decommission services* where the service or provision is not improving sufficiently quickly.

4.79 Among a number of measures to strengthen this role, the Education and Inspections Act 2006 extended the local authority's role in school improvement. Local authorities are now able to issue formal warning notice if they have evidence that a school is coasting, at risk of failure or if children's safety is at risk. This enables the local authority to intervene early, for example by making changes to the governing body of the school, or requiring the school to collaborate with another school or college, to create a more successful instis institution. We shall support Local Authorties to make early and decisive use of these measures.

4.80 This local authority role reflects the fact that the frequency of Ofsted's inspection of schools is differentiated to reflect the relative risks and needs of schools, and it is the local authority who has routine responsibility for seeing where significant risks and underperformance emerge between inspections, and intervening to restore progress. The School Improvement Partner, employed by the local authority, plays a key role in challenging school outside the inspection cycle and for supporting action it takes to improve. The School Improvement Partner's work is led by data about the school, its self-evaluation report and inspection findings, and works closely alongside the Headteacher and with first-hand knowledge of the context. In future, this challenge and support will extend to coasting schools as well as those with very low attainment. This means that even schools with reasonable levels of attainment have to demonstrate that pupils are fulfilling their promise, what ever the ability. As we become better at identifying schools that are coasting and at risk of failure, we are also committed to raising the level of challenge and support from School Improvement Partners, and the confidence of local authorities to invervene quickly to prevent schools sliding into underperformance.

4.81 Local authorities are also taking decisive action to tackle school failure, for example by closing and replacing a failing school, for example with an academy. So far 79 local authorities are working with us on academies and nine local authorities (Manchester, Sunderland, the Corporation of London, Cheshire; Coventry, Kensington and Chelsea, Kent, Telford and Wrekin, and West Sussex) have decided to co-sponsor academies.

4.82 We want to see all local authorities using their new powers to support and challenge schools in their communities to improve and to act early in tackling failing and coasting schools. We will work through the new local government performance framework, which provides more focused and less bureaucratic accountability of local areas to central government and local people, to hold local government to account for delivering excellence across all the schools in their area.

4.83 In Spring 2008 we shall publish to Local Authorities and others engaged in school improvement more details about our approach to school improvement, outlining what we offer to schools and expect from schools at different stages of development, how we intend to sustain the best, encourage the good, challenge the coasting and pull up the weakest schools. And we shall relfect the importance of the local authority role as strategic commissioner of services in revising guidance on Children's Trusts, the Children and Young People's Plans and the role of Director of Children's Services and lead members.

City Challenge

4.84 Building on the success of London Challenge, we will launch City Challenge in 2008, aimed at breaking the cycle of disadvantage and educational underachievement in the Black Country, Greater Manchester and London. It aims over three years to achieve a sharp drop in numbers of underperforming schools, an increase in outstanding schools and significant improvements in educational outcomes for disadvantaged children. The programme will be backed by additional investment and tailored to local needs. It will build on the proven approaches adopted in the capital over the last five years and aims to disseminate best practice to schools in other urban areas.

The right conditions for teaching and learning

4.85 Children need the right environment to be able to learn and thrive. Poor behaviour and other forms of disruption harm the learning of the other children in the classroom. The child misbehaving or truanting puts their future in even greater jeopardy as poor behaviour in school is often a sign of problems later in life. The Children's Plan sets out how we want both to support teachers in improving behaviour in the classroom, and ensure that those children who are disengaged and disaffected are put back on the path to success, not just contained or forgotten.

Behaviour and discipline

4.86 Over the last decade, we have done more than ever before to improve school discipline. Schools have new powers to help them ensure discipline and secure the co-operation of parents, following up the recommendations in *Learning behaviour: Report of the Practitioners' Group on Schools Behaviour and Discipline* chaired by Sir Alan Steer in 2005. In the school year

2006/07 behaviour was judged by Ofsted to be at least satisfactory in almost all primary and secondary schools inspected (over 99 per cent and 98 per cent respectively).

4.87 To help schools raise their game, Ofsted have from September 2007 'raised the bar' on the standards they expect for behaviour and discipline when inspecting schools. Ofsted will mark down any school which has a significant proportion of lessons affected by low level disruption.

4.88 We know from the consultation and other surveys that standards of behaviour at school continue to be a matter of concern for parents, teachers, and children and young people themselves. Satisfactory is not good enough and we need some schools to have even better standards of behaviour and discipline. In order to do this, we are spreading good professional practice and are:

- encouraging local authorities and schools to work with parents to ensure good standards of behaviour, using voluntary parenting contracts for those who need help and support, and using parenting orders for those who are unwilling to engage with improving their child's behaviour; and

- are accelerating the extended school programme in areas of high crime and are encouraging schools to work more closely with other local agencies such as the police and children's services to tackle behaviour problems that affect whole communities such as drugs and gang culture (see Chapter 6).

4.89 We have also asked Sir Alan Steer to review the progress made in the last two years in taking forward the agenda set out in his Practitioner Group's 2005 report for improving school behaviour and discipline. Sir Alan will consider any new issues which need to be addressed as well as give a health check on the Government's implementation of the 2005 recommendations.

Behaviour partnerships

4.90 The Government has set an expectation that all secondary schools should be in behaviour partnerships with a shared commitment to work together to improve behaviour, tackle persistent absence and improve outcomes for children and young people with challenging behaviour. The size of partnerships vary, but they usually consist of about six to ten schools. They operate on the principle that all pupils are the collective responsibility of the partnership and that they will intervene early with children at risk of exclusion and persistent absence.

4.91 Partnerships collaborate and pool resources to offer a range of provision to meet the needs of children with challenging behaviour or additional needs, including on site learning support or nurture units and off site provision such as pupil referral units (PRUs) and tailored courses provided by voluntary and private sector organisations. Although it is early days for these partnerships, they have already shown that this way of working can be effective in reducing the number of permanent exclusions and persistent absentees. We will continue to work with the National Strategies to embed the partnership approach and evaluate its success.

4.92 Sir Alan Steer's report of 2005 recommended that *"the DfES* [now the DCSF] *should require all secondary schools – including academies and foundation schools – to be part of a local partnership and that this should cease to be a voluntary option by 2008"*. Given that 97 per cent of schools are already participating, **we are minded to implement this recommendation and will aks Sir Alan Steer to review progress since his report and the effectiveness of behaviour partnerships** and depending on his findings make participation in the compulsory for all maintained schools and all new academies, encouraging all existing academies to take part as well.

Excluded pupils

4.93 We support unequivocally the right of head teachers to exclude pupils permanently where their behaviour justifies it. But we have also issued new statutory guidance that makes it clear that it is the responsibility of schools, local authorities and carers to work together to reduce the need for exclusion and re-integrate excluded children into the mainstream wherever this is possible. We are particularly concerned about the extent to which permanent exclusion continues to bear disproportionately on certain groups of children and young people, such as Black Caribbean children. We are already working with local authorities and schools to reduce the numbers of exclusions of Black boys. Pupils with SEN are also heavily over-represented among permanently excluded pupils. So **we intend to carry out work with local authorities which have a relatively good record in the area of reducing exclusions of children with SEN, to identify any effective practice which can be shared more widely**.

Improving alternative provision

4.94 We must also improve provision outside schools for excluded pupils and other pupils who for a range of reasons are unable to attend a mainstream school. There are around 70,000 children who receive this kind of provision (0.8 per cent of the pupil population). But while the numbers are relatively small, they include some of our most vulnerable children and young people.

4.95 Local authorities have a duty to ensure these children and young people have urgent access to high quality educational provision. They fulfil this role either as direct providers (through PRUs) or as commissioners of a range of alternative provision from the private and voluntary sector. Schools – either individually or in partnerships – are also commissioners of alternative provision.

4.96 Evidence from Ofsted inspection indicates that while much of this provision is good and some outstanding, there is too much variation in quality. We need to do better if we are to go beyond containing these children – some of whom are the most vulnerable in our society, some of whom will go on to offend and create wider costs to society – and instead help them back on a path to success.

4.97 In order to drive up the quality of alternative provision both for excluded pupils and for others outside mainstream schools, we need to:

- ensure that the accountability of local authorities for the outcomes of children outside mainstream schools really bites;

- take a more robust line on PRUs which offer poor quality provision; and

- develop a greater variety of alternative provision to meet diverse needs by better commissioning and testing alternative models, including studio schools.

4.98 To strengthen the accountability of local authorities for pupils not on a school roll. **We will ask local authorities to collect and publish performance data for pupils not on a school role, to ensure local authorities have incentives to improve their performance**. This information will be published in the School Achievement and Attainment Tables as a separate sub-total for each local authority.

4.99 We shall also expect local authorities to ensure that for every pupil not on a school roll, objectives have been set for educational outcomes, and for the timing of their reintegration into mainstream education where appropriate, and that there are arrangements in place for monitoring progress and for review involving the pupil and his or her parents. This good practice is already followed by many local authorities.

Pupil referral units

4.100 We are already taking action to improve the quality of education offered by PRUs:

- we are requiring them, from February 2008, to have management committees, analogous to school governing bodies. Local head teachers will have a majority on the committees, to ensure that PRUs are more responsive to the priorities of school behaviour partnerships and so have a sharper focus on educational outcomes; and

- we have taken powers to require local authorities, from February 2008, to engage external advisory support for failing PRUs.

4.101 We intend to go beyond this **by introducing new legislation to require local authorities to replace failing PRUs with a specified alternative**. Once we have established the feasibility of high quality alternatives to failing PRUs, we shall use the statutory power to direct local authorities to replace them if they have not been improved after 12 months. We shall also take powers to require local authorities to hold a competition for the replacement PRUs, to bring the intervention regime for PRUs into line with that for mainstream schools.

Other alternative provision

4.102 Children who are disengaged from school, for whatever reason, include some of the young people with the worst prospects for success in later life. The quality of education they recieve is highly variable despite the difference it can make to their prospects. To address this we will drive up the quality of the wider alternative provision market through better informed and more demanding commissioning by:

- developing a national database of providers of alternative provision to be launched in spring 2008, which will give local authority and school partnership commissioners better information on what is available, what outcomes are delivered and what it costs;

- producing improved guidance to commissioners to steer them to look more critically at the relative cost-effectiveness of different providers and the quality of education outcomes obtained; and

- continuing to monitor the performance of school behaviour partnerships and the standard of their commissioning of alternative provision, and to encourage local authorities to do the same.

- **piloting new forms of alternative provision which could include using small schools – studio schools – with close links to business and providing a high quality vocational education**.

4.103 Between them, these measures should stimulate the expansion of the best providers and drive poor quality provision out of the market. We shall set out more details about our proposals for implementing the strategy outlined above for improving the quality of PRUs and alternative provision for wide consultation in early 2008.

Improving school attendance

4.104 Overall school attendance is at its highest recorded level, thanks to a sustained drive over the last few years. We have a good idea of how to promote and sustain regular attendance at individual and school level. But we need to do more to raise aspirations and prevent absence by highlighting the wider opportunities and support we are providing through schools, for example through extended services. Evidence from full service extended schools indicates that behaviour, attendance and motivation all improve.

4.105 A significant minority of children continue to miss large amounts of their schooling. In 2007 just seven per cent of pupils in maintained secondary schools accounted for 32 per cent of all absence and 62 per cent of unauthorised absence in those schools (measured across the autumn and spring terms). Persistent absentees are more likely to have poor educational outcomes and disengage from learning altogether. Although we have succeeded in reducing the number of persistent absentees by ten per cent between 2006 and 2007 there is more to do.

4.106 15 per cent of all absence is unauthorised. Unauthorised absence covers late arrivals and unauthorised term time holidays as well as truancy. Unauthorised absence has risen over the last four years because schools are more resistant to authorising absence, but overall absence has fallen sharply.

4.107 Our aim is to reduce the level of persistent absence by at least a third from 2005/06 levels, so that **by 2011 no local authority will have more than five per cent of its secondary pupils as persistent absentees**. To strengthen the focus of schools in tackling this problem, we shall **include a persistent absence indicator in the School Achievement and Attainment Tables from 2008**.

4.108 To secure this improvement we will deploy the support and challenge functions of the National Strategies, and will require schools to set targets for reducing absence. We will also encourage local authorities and schools to make greater use of measures to secure the co-operation of parents in improving attendance.

Box 4.6: Technology

The developing use of technology is rapidly changing the way our society works and communicates. Children and young people are at the forefront of this, using new media and digital tools effortlessly for supporting learning, their friendships, their creative activity and their entertainment. During the last ten years schools have responded positively to our investment in the use of technology to support teaching and learning and the UK now leads Europe in the extent to which technology is embedded in our schools – but we know from our leading schools that much more can be achieved.

Effective use of technology will underpin many of the activities outlined in the Children's Plan to help us meet the diverse needs of learners and parents, offering them greater choice and flexibility and reduce inequality by:

- ensuring that those who need it most have access to the right technology for learning;

- equipping teachers with the confidence and professional tools they need to support better, more effective learning;

- making sure there are the right conditions for schools and communities to innovate and improve collaboration and sharing of ideas between them;

- breaking down barriers and help communication between schools, families, the learners themselves and the wider community including employers; and

- enabling children and young people to develop the skills they need to use technology well and safely for their future living and learning.

These goals will not be achieved unless we develop a co-ordinated and collaborative effort across all parts of the education system. Becta, the Government's lead agency for technology, will produce additional guidance next year, building on our *Harnessing Technology* strategy, which will outline how this can be done.

World class buildings

4.109 Our unprecedented capital investment programmes are changing the face of education and children's services throughout England. Improvement stretches across the age range – early years and nursery provision, Sure Start Children's Centres and extended services, primary, secondary and special education, youth facilities in and out of school, and 14–19 provision in schools and further education colleges. Over the next three years, we will invest a total of over £23 billion in these services. With over 1,200 new schools and 27,000 classrooms completed, we now have an estimated 675 primary schools and around 1,000 secondary schools in planning for modernisation.

4.110 We began a new strategic approach to investment when we launched Building Schools for the Future in 2003, with the first new secondary school completed in September 2007. Building Schools for the Future has pioneered an approach focused on area-wide education transformation as well as on bricks and mortar. Sure Start followed with a long-term programme to build Sure Start Children's Centres and improve nursery provision. We are now launching the Primary Capital Programme and a Youth Capital Strategy. The importance of capital programmes as a driver of service quality, standards and community cohesion was also acknowledged by the 8–13 Expert Group. We are also setting ourselves the ambitious goal that all new school buildings should be zero carbon by 2016 to contribute to the Government's commitment to reduce carbon emissions.

4.111 Clear local strategic leadership lies at the heart of our approach to each of our capital investment strategies. We work with local authorities to ensure that the vision for improvement is genuinely transformative, that plans are integrated with those for community regeneration to ensure coherence and secure value for money and that all partners in the arrangement have the capacity and skills to deliver the vision for new school buildings.

4.112 Local areas are increasingly co-locating services providing integrated support to children, young people and their families. We will run our capital programmes for early years, schools, youth and 14–19 diploma provision in a simple, coherent and consistent manner to help local agencies to further increase colocation; for example all new schools are being built with the potential for joining up local mainstream services. **We will produce guidance to ensure that where possible new buildings make space for co-located services.** Chapter 7 sets out in more detail our ambition for colocation.

Sustainable environments

4.113 Children and young people are particularly concerned about the environment and climate change.

4.114 Children's Trusts and local authorities also need to ensure that all those services which effect children's lives promote sustainable environments. The Government has already introduced a general duty on local authorities to promote sustainable travel to school. Our aim is also for all schools to be sustainable schools by 2020. We want all newly built schools to reduce carbon emissions by at least 60 per cent.

4.115 In the Children's Plan we will take our aspiration one step further by **setting an ambition for all new school buildings to be zero carbon by 2016**. We know that with the technologies currently available, the zero carbon ambition cannot be achieved on many school sites. It is a challenge for all those involved in the design and construction of new buildings to develop new technologies to deliver increasingly low carbon buildings. We are therefore appointing a taskforce to advise on how to achieve zero carbon schools, whether the timescale is realistic and how to reduce carbon emissions in the intervening period. The taskforce will work closely with designers, builders, local authorities and other key stakeholders to develop a road map to zero carbon schools.

Box 4.7: Sustainable schools

Sustainable development is a non-negotiable for children's wellbeing. At Cassop Primary School, winners of the 2007 Teaching Award for Sustainable Schools, children believe that they can make a difference to their world. The 'Green Team' pupils ensure their school reduces carbon emissions – making sure lights are turned off and energy is saved, recycling paper and growing their own vegetables. The school has a wind turbine, solar panels, and heating which runs on recycled wood pellets.

Young people across the country are using the Carbon Detectives Kit to investigate their school's carbon footprint and take action to reduce it. Many are taking up the We Are What We Do's challenge to come up with actions to change the world. The work of school councils, of eco-teams, and young people undertaking positive activities in their communities is a hugely powerful driver for sustainable development. As adults we have a responsibility to look ahead and find solutions that improve the quality of children's lives without storing up problems that they will have to address in the future. One sure way to do this is to empower our children to change their environment.

Conclusion

4.116 This chapter sets out our plans for a world-class early years and schools workforce, operating in a diverse and collaborative system, backed by clear governance and accountability arrangements, where children and young people learn in inspiring and high quality environments. Alongside the steps highlighted in this Chapter we will also revise the Delivery Agreements for PSAs 10 and 11 in co-operation with other departments. These are also the elements which contribute to the ambition set out in Chapter 5 to ensure that all young people are participating and achieving their potential up to the age of 18 and beyond.

Chapter 5: Staying on

Ensure young people are participating and achieving their potential to 18 and beyond

Executive summary

5.1 A changing economy means we need to ensure our children and young people have the right skills as they become adults and move into further or higher education, or into work. By 2015, we want all young people to stay on in education or training to 18 and beyond. And when they leave we want them to have the skills they need to prosper in a high skills economy.

5.2 To achieve this we must reduce the numbers who are not in education, employment and training. Diplomas and Apprenticeships will increase the learning options available to 14–19-year-olds and will also help tackle the concerns raised by employers and higher education institutes about the broader functional and personal, learning and thinking skills of learners. To reinforce the impact of 14–19 reform, we will:

- legislate in this Parliamentary session to raise the participation age to 17 from 2013 and 18 from 2015;

- develop 3 new Diplomas in science, humanities and languages to increase the options for young people;

- create a new independent regulator of qualifications, with the consultation launched before the end of 2007;

- transfer funding for 16–19 learning from the Learning and Skills Council to local authorities, with a consultation on how best to achieve this in early 2008; and

- allocate £31.5 million over the next three years on a new programme to re-engage 16-year-olds who are not currently engaged in learning, building on the extra measures we have announced on NEETs, including better tracking and financial incentives to remain in learning.

Vision for the next decade

5.3 By the end of the next decade, the Government wants all young people to stay on in education or training to 18 and beyond. And when they leave we want them to have the skills they need to prosper in a high skills economy. This way, we will build national wealth and tackle deprivation and poverty. We can only achieve this by changing the expectations and aspirations of young people, their parents, and the education and training system. Because aspirations are passed from parent to child, increased participation and achievement by one generation will raise aspiration and participation for the next.

5.4   To underline our commitment to this vision, our ambition is for, **by 2020, every young person to have the skills for adult life and further study, with at least 90 per cent achieving the equivalent of five higher level GCSEs by age 19, and 70 per cent achieveing the equivalent of 2 A levels by age 19**. We will also improve young people's 'softer' skills, which employers tell us are so important. Our aim is that by 2020 young people will have much stronger functional, personal, learning and thinking skills so that **employers are satisfied with young people's readiness to work.**

5.5   We have just agreed three Public Service Agreements (PSAs), which help contribute to achieving this ambition: to raise the educational achievement of all children and young people (PSA 10), to narrow the gap in educational achievement between children in disadvantaged groups and their peers (PSA 11), and to increase the number of children and young people on the path to success (PSA 14). For young people aged 14–19, these will be measured in the following ways:

- PSA 10: increasing the proportion achieving Level 5 in both English and mathematics at Key Stage 3, increasing the proportion of young people achieving five A*–C GCSEs (or equivalent) including GCSEs in both English and mathematics, and increasing the proportion of young people achieving Level 2 and Level 3 at 19;

- PSA 11: the proportion of pupils progressing by two levels in English and mathematics at Key Stages 3 and 4, and closing the gap between the initial participation in full-time higher education rates for young people aged 18, 19 and 20 from the top three and bottom four socio-economic classes; and

- PSA 14: reducing the percentage of 16–18-year-olds not in education, employment or training.

5.6   In the longer term, as set out in the Green Paper *Raising Expectations: staying in education and training post-16,* **by 2013 young people will stay in education and training until the end of the academic year in which they turn 17, and by 2015 until their 18th birthday.**

Key areas for reform

5.7   We are in the process of transforming our system of 14–19 education to support our ambition. Most young people who currently do not stay in education say this is because the right provision is not available or they do not have the qualifications to progress. We want to create a system focused on high standards and – in line with our vision of a system with the needs of children and young people at the forefront – much more tailored to the talents and aspirations of young people as individuals. Further education has a key role to play in delivering our ambition for world class skills. Focusing on delivering the skills employers need, it operates across society and has a real impact on the lives of people from disadvantaged and minority communities.

5.8   Action in three areas will help deliver our objectives:

a. **increasing support** for those already in the system to stay in learning, by getting them onto the right programmes, providing them with financial support, and helping them to achieve;

b. **reforming curriculum and qualifications** to give young people more choice and flexibility and to make sure that what young people learn is relevant and engaging. Central to this is the introduction of Diplomas, and the development of functional skills, which will be at the heart of all qualification routes; and

c. **delivering on the ground** by ensuring that everyone involved in working with 14–19-year-olds group works together to take a strategic view of young people's needs, to provide them with their full entitlement and to offer a personalised approach to their learning.

5.9 We have set out the details of the reforms we are undertaking to achieve our goals in our 2005 White Paper *14–19 Education and Skills*. In March 2007 in the Green Paper *Raising Expectations* we explained further how the reforms (complemented by legislation) would help us to achieve our aim to have all young people participating in full- or part-time education or training by 2015. That legislation is now going through Parliament and will take effect from 2013, alongside the new entitlement to Diplomas and Apprenticeships. This chapter sets out the action we are taking to deliver our ambitions.

Families

5.10 As young people grow older, they take increasing responsibility for themselves. Nonetheless, parental support remains crucial. Parents are the key influence on the choices young people make at age 14 and 16. The Government needs to help parents to understand the new options becoming available, including new entitlements to Diplomas and Apprenticeships, and make sure that they are able to offer advice in a system that will have changed considerably since they were at school and college. As we raise the participation age, young people themselves will be responsible for participating, but parents will be expected to provide support and assistance.

Increasing support

5.11 The latest participation data shows an increase in the proportion of 17-year-olds who are participating in education and work-based learning of 1.4 percentage points in 2006 to 77.5 per cent, the highest ever rate. We have also made good progress on the number of young people achieving Level 2 qualifications, with over 71 per cent of young people aged 19 being qualified to at least Level 2 in 2006. Our target is to raise this to 85 per cent by 2013. At the same time we have finally begun to make some inroads into the percentage of young people who are not in education, employment or training. Further education colleges are more successful than ever, with success rates rising from 55 per cent in 1999/2000 to 77 per cent in 2005/06, and more young people are succeeding in Apprenticeships – 63 per cent having achieved a full framework so far in 2006/07 increasing from 24 per cent in 2001/02. However, there remain significant and sustained gaps in participation in post-16 full-time education and training, based on gender, ethnicity, social class and region.

5.12 A number of reforms are contributing to improving participation and attainment:

- the September Guarantee – a commitment that all young people should be made an offer of learning by the end of the September after they complete Year 11 – has ensured that in 2007 almost every 16-year-old has been offered an appropriate place in education or training;

- we have provided support to those who need it, designed to meet their needs, in areas with particularly low levels of participation or attainment;

- the Educational Maintenance Allowance has provided a financial incentive for young people from disadvantaged backgrounds to remain in education and training post-16;

- we are testing out further financial support for those who are not in education, employment or training;

- we are introducing post-16 progression measures that will ensure all providers are focused on the needs of each young person, whatever level they have achieved so far; and

- reforms in Key Stage 4 are providing a better range of applied qualifications to keep more young people engaged and prospering in education.

5.13   However, there is still more to do to ensure that all children and young people have access to the information and the support they need for their individual circumstances.

Information, advice and guidance

5.14   The importance of high quality information, advice and guidance (IAG) was emphasised by our 14–19 Expert Group, which recommended a focus on supporting young people through transitions. It also emphasised the need for sources of, and access to, IAG being seamless across the whole age range. The importance of IAG was also reflected in the *Time to Talk* consultation where one in four young people mentioned education services as their best experience of support, direct feedback indicating that this was both academic and emotional support.

> "In school when I needed adult support to help me through emotional times, my head of year and others were there."

> "School nurse who supports us confidentially with our worries/personal problems."

> "More talk about information we want to know about."

> *(Findings from young people, Time to Talk consultation)*

5.15   As young people move towards adulthood, they face a range of challenges which require them to make difficult life and learning choices. They need help to understand their options and to make informed decisions, especially as we increase the range of learning options available to young people. It will be even more important after we have raised the participation age as we know that learners who receive good quality IAG are less likely to drop out of learning or change course after they turn 16.

5.16   IAG is an umbrella term that covers a range of activities that help young people to become more self-reliant and better equipped to manage their own learning and personal and career development. Young people particularly value support and advice from other young people and opportunities to experience the options available to them – including 'taster' provision, which enables young people to experience the sorts of activity they would do on different learning programmes. We will expect these forms of guidance – peer advice and mentoring, and opportunities for tasters and other 'experiential learning' to be available to young people across the country.

5.17 We will expect 14–19 partnerships to take responsibility for ensuring that all young people in an area have these opportunities. The partnership will provide the forum in which schools, colleges and other providers can agree how between them, they will ensure that all learners within their institutions have appropriate access to such opportunities, and receive impartial advice and guidance, including the opportunity to understand the courses and other provision which is available at other institutions in their area. From April 2008, local authorities will be responsible for commissioning and managing IAG services in their areas. The 14–19 partnership is convened by the local authority and will include the local authority's provider of Connexions services. Schools and colleges should agree through the partnership how the independent service they provide will be used to supplement what is available within the school – and can be used to inform and support the staff delivering guidance on careers and future learning opportunities. Parent support and advice services in local authorities also have an important role to play, and we will work with them to ensure that they offer support to parents wanting to help and advise their children.

5.18 At present, the quality of IAG falls short of what young people need. To remedy this we have published quality standards that set out our expectations of the IAG services that local authorities will provide. The 14–19 consortia that will be delivering Diplomas in 2008 have had to pass through a rigorous process in order to ensure they will deliver high quality, comprehensive and impartial information, advice and guidance. In future, there will be an annual report back from the Diploma Gateway process summarising the progress made in establishing effective provision.

5.19 The 2007 Budget announced that schools should provide every young person with a learning guide (see Chapter 3) who will support them to make good progress across all subjects as well as developing as an individual. They will work with young people to identify their long-term aspirations and guide them on the best choice of subjects at age 14 and 16. As we pilot learning guides, we will test how they can help young people to find out about activities available through extended schools and to look to future education, training and career choices. For care leavers, who are particularly at risk both of not participating in education, employment or training, and of engaging in risky behaviours, the Children and Young Persons Bill will extend the entitlement to a personal adviser up to the age of 25 for all care leavers who are either in education or wish to return to education.

5.20 To drive up the quality of careers education in schools, the Education and Skills Bill will require schools to provide impartial information and advice on learning and careers options. We will help schools by developing guidance for the new personal, social, health and economic curriculum. We will also fund a project to explore the impact of early careers interventions at Key Stage 2 in extending horizons and raising aspirations, and we will develop guidance to give young people more opportunities for experiential learning. Peers can play an important role in mentoring other young people, and we will encourage wider and more effective use of peer mentoring and provide mentors with better support.

5.21 Another important source of information for young people about learning opportunities is 14–19 area prospectuses. These allow young people, supported by their parents or a trusted adult, to make informed choices about where and how they would like to undertake their learning.

5.22 The need for IAG does not change dramatically once someone reaches the age of 19. Good quality IAG needs to be seamless across all age ranges, and is increasingly important to ensure coherence and smoother transitions between youth and adult services. We will set out our plans for improving links between services for young people and for adults in early 2008.

5.23 The voluntary and community sector plays a central role in the delivery of specialist IAG services, for example on drugs and sexual health. Together with local authorities, we will explore what support they need to work more effectively, and how we can support the professional development of their advisers.

Helping young people not in education, employment or training

5.24 The regional patterns for young people who are not in education, employment or training (NEET) show that the highest rates are in areas which have lost traditional industries like coalmining or shipbuilding. Even though alternative employment opportunities may be available, low aspirations and low skills have become entrenched. As the UK economy continues to adjust, those young people that remain disengaged will become progressively more marginalised, as non-participation is a strong predictor of later unemployment, low incomes, teenage parenthood, depression, and poor physical health.

5.25 We know also that certain groups are most at risk of becoming NEET, including young people with learning difficulties or disabilities, teenage mothers, young offenders and care leavers.

5.26 In late 2007 the Government published the NEET strategy, aimed to reduce sharply the proportion of young people not in education, employment or training by:

- careful tracking to identify early those young people who are NEET, or who are at risk of becoming NEET. In particular, we will be requiring all learning providers to notify the Connexions service as soon as any young person drops out;

- personalised guidance and support to make sure young people know how to access education, training or employment and tailoring some intensive support for those who have more complex needs;

- providing a full range of courses to meet demand. We will be extending the September Guarantee to 17-year-olds, and ensuring that where young people drop out of education they are given the support to re-engage, reflecting what the 14–19 Expert Group told us; and

- introducing a new emphasis on rights and responsibilities. All young people who have been NEET for at least 26 weeks by the time they reach their 18th birthday are fast-tracked to the intensive support and sanctions regime of the New Deal. This will be voluntary from April 2008 and mandatory from April 2009.

5.27 **We are legislating in this Parliamentary session to raise the participation age to 17 from 2013 and to 18 from 2015.** The strategy will ensure that ahead of 2013 we can be confident of having engaged many more young people in learning and work that presently would not be engaged.

Case study: Westfield School, Watford

The 6th form support worker works closely with the Connexions personal adviser, meeting monthly to discuss the needs of individual students, in particular those at risk of dropping out. They communicate regularly by email and telephone and immediately when the support worker becomes aware a young person has left the institution so that the young person can be quickly followed up.

5.28   In addition, **we will allocate £31.5 million over three years to a new programme designed to re-engage those who are not currently engaged in learning post-16**. A number of innovative voluntary sector and local authority funded schemes have succeeded here by restoring young people's confidence and self-esteem. However, the connections between schemes of this kind and more formal learning programmes funded by the Learning and Skills Council may not be strong. Our new entry to learning programme will bridge this gap by ensuring that re-enagement is accompanied by clear and personalised progression routes which will take them step by step back into formal learning. Young people will be supported through mentoring to move from good quality re-engagement activities through semi-formal personal development and other learning back into more formal learning, through steps they can manage. This will ensure that more young people are given opportunities to succeed in education and training, and that – as we move to raise the participation age – all young people are offered routes that work for them post-16.

Financial support

5.29   Our vision is to provide a financial support system that will attract and retain young people in learning. At the heart of this is the Education Maintenance Allowance (EMA), a £500 million programme aimed at supporting young people from disadvantaged backgrounds to stay in education. The EMA offers 'something for something' – to gain financial support students must agree and stick to a contract for attendance and achievement with their school or college.

5.30   Eligibility is designed to support young people from low income families, and young people in other disadvantaged groups such as young offenders, Gypsy, Roma and Traveller children, and children in care. Teenage parents are assessed on their own income, with support for childcare costs available through the Care to Learn scheme to help them continue with their learning.

5.31   Over 527,000 young people benefited from EMA payments in 2006/07, and around 45 per cent of learners aged 16–18 in full-time education currently receive EMA. We have extended the use of EMA to a wider range of courses, so more young people can benefit. Research from the EMA pilots suggests that the introduction of EMA has led to increases in participation nationally by 3.8 percentage points for 16-year-olds and 4.1 percentage points for 17-year-olds.

5.32   To remove financial barriers and raise aspiration, from the 2008/09 academic year 16-year-olds who qualify for an EMA will be guaranteed a minimum level of maintenance support if they decide to go into higher education. For students already in higher education, there are a number of different sources of financial help available including student loans, maintenance grants and university bursaries. In 2008/09 it is expected that around two thirds of all new full-time students will be eligible for a maintenance grant worth up to £2,835 per year. Through the Children and Young Persons Bill we will introduce a national bursary of a minimum of £2,000 for all care leavers who enter higher education.

Reforming curriculum and qualifications

5.33 If all young people are to participate and achieve to age 19, the Government needs to provide a choice of routes which can motivate all young people and help them progress to further learning and employment. The curriculum must be more relevant and work related, whilst continuing to focus on the basics.

5.34 Key to achieving this is the introduction of Diplomas, which combine academic and applied learning. They will sit alongside expanded Apprenticeships, which give young people the opportunity to work for an employer, learn on the job, build up knowledge and transferable skills, and gain nationally recognised qualifications for working life. A levels are being improved to reduce the assessment burden, introduce more stretching and challenging assessment approaches, and introduce an A* grade to reward the very best performers.

5.35 We are developing a foundation learning tier to bring together a range of smaller qualifications into a more coherent stage and to provide clearer progression routes.

5.36 Whichever route they take, we want all young people to have the functional skills in English, mathematics and ICT they need in order to be successful in work and life. Young people taking Diplomas will develop better personal, learning and thinking skills. The new extended project at Level 3 will also help young people develop their research and critical thinking skills.

5.37 We are currently implementing a range of measures to increase the number of young people studying science, technology, engineering and mathematics (see Chapter 4). These subjects are key to the nation's competitiveness. And improving young people's language skills is important as we move towards an increasingly global economy.

5.38 Underpinning these reforms, we plan to create a new independent regulator of qualifications and tests in order to maintain public confidence in the rigour of our qualifications.

Diplomas

5.39 Diplomas will directly address the UK's urgent skills need. By combining theory and practical skills with first hand experience and insight into the world of work, they will help young people to develop a rigorous and practical knowledge of one or more business sectors – for example engineering – and also subject disciplines such as languages, science and humanities. Diplomas will be available at three levels – foundation, intermediate, and advanced.

5.40 For a number of years, employers have been saying that they need more young people leaving education with the basics of English and mathematics, but also employability skills, such as the ability to communicate well and to work in a team. Higher education institutions have been saying that young people need to start higher education with better research, independent study and critical thinking skills. Diplomas are a response to these challenges.

5.41 Employers and universities are playing a key role in determining the content of each Diploma so the value of Diplomas will be guaranteed.

5.42 The success of the Increased Flexibility Programme, Young Apprenticeships and other initiatives that open up the range of choices for young people has shown us that young people of all abilities benefit from the opportunity to undertake practical-based, work-related learning. Options around additional and specialist learning will enable learners to put together personalised programmes of varying breadth and depth – qualifications which work around them and do not require them to fit into a set mould.

5.43 Consortia of schools, colleges and other learning providers will begin delivering the first five Diplomas from September 2008. A further five will be rolled out from September 2009, and four more in September 2010. By 2013, all students anywhere in the country will be able to choose one of the first 14 Diplomas.

5.44 In October 2007 the Government **announced the introduction of three new Diplomas in science, humanities and languages**. We expect that these will become available for first teaching in September 2011. Diploma development partnership structures will shortly be established to specify the content for each of these new Diplomas, and will include representatives from employers and higher education as well as from schools, colleges, and subject associations.

5.45 In 2013 we will review the evidence and experience following the introduction of all Diplomas to examine how the overall offer meets the needs of young people in progressing to further study and employment. This will be the first full review, following the implementation of the new entitlement, of the range of qualifications available to 14–19 year olds, in the light of experience of uptake and the views of young people, parents, schools, colleges, employers and univesities.

> *"The Diploma in IT offers an exciting way for students to learn and apply their skills in business–relevant ways. At Microsoft, we welcome initiatives that seek to increase the level of IT skills for young people leaving school and entering the workforce or moving on to university." (Steve Beswick – Director of Education, Microsoft Ltd)*

Apprenticeships

5.46 Both Diplomas and Apprenticeships offer choice and flexibility, with Apprenticeships providing occupational training for young people seeking to enter a specific area of employment. This complements the broader sector-based programme of study offered by Diplomas which could lead to specialisation further down the track.

5.47 Young Apprenticeships currently provide 14–16-year-olds with a range of applied qualifications through learning programmes that include a strong emphasis on practical and work-based learning, with 50 days work experience over two years. From September 2008 we will be trialling delivery of Young Apprenticeships with Diplomas as the underpinning qualifications.

5.48 We are planning to expand post-16 Apprenticeships even further – the numbers having already increased from 75,000 in 1997 to 250,000 in 2007. The Apprenticeships entitlement for all school leavers who meet the entry criteria will apply from 2013, in line with the entitlement to study any one of the first 14 Diplomas. These commitments move us towards offering 400,000 Apprenticeships in 2020 – responding to the challenges set out in the Leitch Review of Skills. A review of Apprenticeships, due to report in January 2008, is currently considering what more can be done to make progress towards this ambition.

Functional skills

5.49 We want all young people to develop and be recognised for the skills to operate confidently, effectively and independently in life and at work. That is why we are making functional skills in English, mathematics and ICT a core part of 14–19 qualifications. Functional skills are not simply about knowledge in these subjects, but crucially about knowing when and how to use the knowledge in real life contexts. Functional skills assessments are currently being piloted and will be available across England from September 2010. In order to get a Diploma, learners will need to gain all three functional skills at the appropriate level. New mathematics, English and ICT GCSEs are being developed for first teaching in 2010. In order to get grade A*–C in these new GCSEs, learners will also need to pass Level 2 functional skills in the relevant subject.

A levels and GCSEs

5.50 The Government is also reforming GCSEs and A levels so that they continue to represent relevant and high quality qualifications. At GCSE, the introduction of controlled assessment in place of coursework will address concerns about the way tasks are set and marked, and new GCSEs in English, mathematics and ICT from 2010 will be linked to achievement of functional skills as set out above.

5.51 At A level, we are reducing the assessment burden by reducing the number of modules in the majority of subjects from six to four. A level specifications have also been revised to introduce greater stretch and challenge: from 2008, young people will study A levels which will contain more open ended questions, requiring greater thought and more detailed written replies. We are also introducing a new A* grade to reward the very best performance, encouraging our brightest students to demonstrate the upper limits of their ability. And we are introducing a new Extended Project, which can be taken alongside A levels or as part of the Advanced Diploma, which will give students a chance to develop and demonstrate skills of independent research and critical thinking.

Foundation learning tier

5.52 Young people of all abilities should be able to access suitable learning routes. The foundation learning tier is intended to meet the needs of young people and adults, particularly some of those with learning difficulties or disabilities, who will benefit from taking entry level qualifications before moving onto a higher level of study and achievement, or who will benefit from taking longer to study for qualifications at entry level or Level 1. A feature of the foundation learning tier will be the establishment of progression pathways – clear stepping stones that will help learners to access a first full Level 2 programme or to develop the skills necessary for living independently. The entry level pathway for 14–16-year-olds will be piloted on a small scale from September 2008 and full implementation will be complete by 2010.

Personal learning and thinking skills

5.53 As set out in Chapter 3, in addition to the basics, we want all young people to develop a wider set of skills, whichever educational route they are on. As set out above, employers have told us that they want to see a greater focus on 'employability' skills. Our higher education partners have also told us that young people need to be stronger in independent study and research skills. In response to these demands, the Qualifications and Curriculum Authority has developed a framework of personal, learning and thinking skills for learning, work and life. This has been used to embed the development of these skills throughout the revised secondary curriculum and within Diplomas.

5.54 This need to focus on the development of a wider skills set was reflected in the 14–19 Expert Group discussions, where it was agreed that there should be a greater focus on the development of 'soft' skills, relationship skills, and critical thinking skills through school and college activity. Some respondents to the *Time to Talk* consultation also felt that education could be improved to better prepare children and young people for adult life.

> *"Secondary schools should teach all children 'life skills' which will help them to obtain worthwhile jobs when they leave."*
> *(Female, Reading – Time to Talk consultation)*

> *"Employers need literate, numerate young people with a positive attitude, who are able to communicate effectively, work in teams and have good business awareness. The new Diplomas, designed with these needs in mind, should ensure young people develop vital literacy, numeracy and employability skills, and apply them in real-life situations to help them see the relevance for their future working lives. Diplomas will also provide students with a valuable understanding about the ways particular sectors operate."*
> *(Richard Lambert – Director General, CBI)*

Science, technology, engineering and mathematics

5.55 We are currently implementing a range of measures to ensure enough young people with higher level science, technology, engineering and mathematics (STEM) skills to meet the economic needs of the UK. The new Diplomas will include a number, such as engineering, ICT, and the sciences, that will help to develop STEM skills. We want to see more young people studying and enjoying STEM subjects so that more continue to study them post-16 through to first degree level and beyond. We have set challenging targets for recruiting and retaining subject specialist teachers, for improvement in attainment at Key Stage 3 and GCSEs, and the number of young people taking science and mathematics A levels (see also Chapter 4).

5.56 We have reformed the science and mathematics secondary curriculum to make it more engaging, relevant and practical, and we are supporting schools to widen access to the opportunity to study triple science GCSE (biology, chemistry and physics as separate GCSEs). We are supporting schools to develop science and engineering clubs with business engagement. We are investing in a range of measures to encourage more young people to continue to study STEM subjects beyond 16, including a major communications and careers guidance campaign. This will help raise awareness of the range of career opportunities to which studying STEM subjects can lead.

5.57 As part of our work to improve the effectiveness of support for STEM we are developing new arrangements to bring together the very large number of STEM support schemes into a coherent framework, aligned to national priorities and to improve the signposting of support available for schools and colleges.

Languages

5.58 The ability to communicate in languages other than English is becoming increasingly important. We are implementing recommendations made by Lord Dearing earlier in 2007 to increase the number of young people studying languages post-14. These include further embedding language learning in the primary curriculum, making the secondary curriculum more engaging and relevant, providing more support for teachers and wider use of the Languages Ladder to recognise young people's achievement. The new languages Diploma will offer an attractive new option to keep young people in language learning.

Securing confidence in the curriculum, qualifications and tests

5.59 The Qualifications and Curriculum Authority (QCA) currently has a wide ranging role. It is responsible to ministers for monitoring, developing and advising on the curriculum. Its regulatory arm also regulates National Curriculum tests and accredits qualifications for both young people and adults.

5.60 QCA has demonstrated independence in its work as a regulator and has developed a system for assuring standards that is internationally recognised for its quality and reliability. However, having the same body involved in the design and development of qualifications, and the regulation of the qualifications system, may lead to a perceived conflict of interest which could undermine confidence in standards.

5.61 We therefore propose to create a new independent regulator which will report directly to Parliament on the standards of qualifications and tests. **Consultation on this proposal, and on the consequential changes to the QCA, will start later this month and run until March 2008.** Our intention is to establish an interim regulatory body from April 2008. We will introduce legislation to establish the new bodies at the earliest opportunity.

Delivering on the ground

5.62 It is not sufficient simply to offer new qualifications. The Government also needs to be confident that they are being delivered effectively on the ground to provide greater opportunities for achievement and progression. The principle of services collaborating around the needs of the child or young person that forms a central part of this Plan's vision is critical here if learners are to have access to the full range of curriculum and qualification options. Alongside this, we need to focus on 14–19 workforce development to ensure that the workforce is trained to provide a high quality and relevant learning experience. The development of National Digital Infrastructure will help facilitate collaboration, setting out the role that technology can and should play to support delivery (see also Chapter 4).

Collaborative delivery

5.63 By 2013, every young person aged 14–19 will be entitled to study whichever of the 14 new Diplomas they choose, at whatever level is appropriate for them. This entitlement goes well beyond what would be possible for any one school or college to offer alone. We know that offering young people a range of learning environments can help them to develop confidence and new skills, as well as motivate those who are at risk of disengagement. Therefore, we are asking schools, colleges and other providers to work together to offer more than any one of them could by acting alone. Consortia of schools, colleges, work-based learning providers, employers, Connexions services and others are being formed across the country to offer Diplomas and – in many cases – other qualifications as well. 149 such consortia have passed through a quality control process known as the Gateway to offer the first five Diplomas in September 2008, and the second Gateway process is now underway to determine who will offer Diplomas from September 2009. National skills academies will build the capacity of the further education system to respond to employer needs, and will offer access to innovative skills provision right through to higher level technical skills at Level 3 and Level 4+ – we are on target to have 12 national skills academies by the end of 2008.

5.64 In order to take a more strategic view of provision and to promote better integration of 14–19 services, 14–19 partnerships have been set up in every local authority area, some led by the local authority and others by the Learning and Skills Council. The partnerships vary in terms of geographical size and membership, but all play an essential role in supporting the work of the local Children's Trust.

5.65 At the same time as the Department for Children, Schools and Families (DCSF) was created, it was announced that the funding for the education of 16–19-year-olds would be transferred from the Learning and Skills Council to local authorities, signalling a fundamental change in the 16–19 education system.

5.66 Effective planning to meet the needs of young people can only happen locally. The transfer of funding to local authorities means that leadership of the system, accountability for outcomes, discharge of duties and the management of funding to deliver will all happen at a local level. This reflects the vital role we have set out for local authorities in leading improvement for all aspects of children's and young people's lives.

5.67 **In early 2008 the Department for Innovation, Universities and Skills (DIUS) and DCSF will consult jointly on our proposals for how the system will work under these new arrangements, both before and after age 19.** This will include regional events to make sure those who have a personal or professional interest will be able to participate in the consultation process. The joint consultation will be set alongside the review of schools funding which is planned for spring 2008. Decision making will be underpinned by the principles recently set out in a letter that was sent jointly by Ministers from DCSF and DIUS to the further education sector stating that:

- decision making, accountability and funding rules must be transparent and equitable;
- they must have a clear focus on quality and respect our aim that the quality of the learner's experience is our ultimate goal;
- they must make sure the funding follows the learner's choice;

- they need to respect our aim that providers of all types can benefit from processes which are as simple and straightforward as possible, and which provide coherence for providers which span different areas and age groups;

- they must secure for providers greater autonomy to act on behalf of learners within the national frameworks, and ensure that any intervention is proportionate to under-performance; and

- they must secure good value for money in the allocation and use of public funds.

5.68 A key part of this consultation will be about the national role. For example, only at a national level can we deliver learner support, manage the data systems and administer funding. There is a quality and monitoring role which must be consistent with the national indicator set and the Local Government White Paper.

5.69 Raising aspiration can be a significant motivator in raising attainment. Efforts to raise aspirations will stem from DCSF's system leadership role which will promote the motivation and engagement of all children and young people and the development of a better quality workforce. Higher education is a key partner in raising ambition and aspiration working collaboratively in schools.

5.70 DIUS and DCSF jointly published a prospectus for higher education in October 2007 to encourage institutions to establish more formal partnerships through sponsoring academies or supporting trust schools, and we are exploring more broadly what universities and colleges can do to extend, strengthen and sustain effective relationships with schools (see also Chapter 4). Higher education institutions already work in partnership with schools through successful programmes such as Aimhigher and the Student Associate Scheme. Aimhigher enables local partnerships of higher education institutions, schools and colleges to co-design and deliver a range of activity which can raise the attainment and aspiration levels of young people from backgrounds currently under-represented in higher education.

14–19 workforce reform

5.71 The suite of 14–19 reforms set out in this chapter aim to give young people the opportunity to pursue a wider range of options, which will engage them in new styles of learning and equip them more effectively for work and study. But successful delivery of Diplomas and other reforms will depend upon the capability of the workforce. We want to do more to facilitate effective joint working between the workforce in schools and the further education sector. To do this we will provide more professional development opportunities and explore how we can make interchange between the sectors easier, including identifying where differences in regulations and qualifications appear to set unnecessary barriers.

5.72 Currently, the mainstream system for training school and further education teachers does not include a specific 14–19 component, and we urgently need to address the lack of sector-specific and industrial knowledge of most school teaching staff. Further education teachers tend to have more experience in this area, but although improvements have been realised in recent years, have usually had less training and support to develop skills in personalisation and pedagogy for 14–16-year-olds. We need to address these specific skills gaps for individual members of staff, and increase the collaborative capacity of institutions and individuals to bring in and deploy particular expertise to offer a complete and high quality package of tuition for every young person.

5.73 In the future, the skills needed for 14–19 reforms will need to form part of initial teacher training and continuing professional development for both schools and the further education sector, so that practitioners have clear progression and professional qualification routes. This should give young people more choice and flexibility about their particular course of study and ensure that they are not hampered by professional boundaries.

5.74 We are currently consulting on a workforce strategy for further education, to be published shortly. The strategy is looking at how we make the workforce more professional, and ensure we are recruiting and retaining the right people while developing the existing workforce. The equality and diversity of the workforce is at the heart of the strategy. These reforms – a new professional status for teachers, and new qualifications and professional development for them and principals – will ensure that courses will meet the needs of learners and employers.

5.75 Alongside the strategy, we are conducting a priority review into the 14–19 workforce development. This reflects the recommendations of the 14–19 Expert Group, which suggested a review of current demands on workers in the system, with a particular focus on developing a greater understanding of the roles of individuals and the skills they require to fulfil their roles effectively.

Conclusion

5.76 Skill development needs to start early – well before young people enter the workforce, or even start to train for specific occupations. The reforms set out in this chapter illustrate how young people will be offered choice, and be supported in their choices, to help them to remain engaged up to the age of 18 and beyond. Chapter 6 looks more widely at our vision for all young people to enjoy happy, healthy and safe teenage years that prepare them well for adult life – keeping them on the path to success.

Chapter 6: On the right track

Keep children and young people on the path to success

Executive summary

6.1   We want all young people to enjoy happy, healthy and safe teenage years and to be prepared for adult life. Too often we focus on the problems of a few young people rather than the successes of the many – we want a society where young people feel valued and in which their achievements are recognised and celebrated.

6.2   Positive activities and experiences are a vital part of happy and enjoyable teenage years. We have established a Youth Task Force to ensure that we improve delivery of young people's services and so that they are designed around their needs. We have already announced investment of £60 million in improving youth facilities in advance of funding released from unclaimed assets. But we want further and faster transformation of the lives of young people and so we will:

- invest £160 million over the next three years to improve the quality and range of places for young people to go and things for them to do;

- develop an entitlement for all young people to participate in positive activities which develop their talents including piloting a new offer to take part in cultural activities in and out of school; and

- spend £20 million over the next three years to use Acceptable Behaviour Contracts as a measure to prevent young people engaging in antisocial behaviour and to ensure young people receive support to improve their behaviour at the same time as an Antisocial Behaviour Order.

6.3   Experimentation in early teenage years and adolescence can expose young people to risks, and where they fail to make informed and sensible choices, they can too often put their health and future at stake. To tackle behaviour that puts young people at risk and help young people manage these risks, we will:

- publish a youth alcohol action plan in spring 2008, around the same time as the new Drugs Strategy which will:
  - improve alcohol education in schools;
  - tackle parental alcohol misuse which can influence young people's own consumption; and
  - consider the case for further action on alcohol advertising.

6.4 Following Expert Group discussions of the importance of relationships as young people move from adolescence to adulthood we will:

- review best practice in effective sex and relationships education and how it is delivered in schools.

6.5 The majority of young people do not offend but we need to reduce the harm caused by youth crime both to those who are victims and to young offenders themselves. In advance of the Youth Crime Action Plan, the Children's Plan sets out how we want mainstream services to work together to prevent crime, what we will do to deal swiftly with those involved in youth crime and how we will prevent reoffending including:

- allocating, with the Home Office, £66 million over the next three years to target those most at risk;

- piloting a restorative approach to youth offenders; and

- publishing a Green Paper in 2008 looking at what happens when young offenders leave custody and consult on how to improve the education they receive in custody.

Vision for the next decade

6.6 As we have set out in the earlier chapters of the Children's Plan, achieving our vision of success for all young people means putting in place the right opportunities and support so that they:

- succeed in education and learning;

- develop resilience and wider social and emotional skills;

- can make a real contribution to their communities and wider society;

- are physically, mentally and emotionally healthy; and

- grow up in a safe and supportive environment.

6.7 The Government's vision for the next decade is underpinned by our new PSA to increase the number of children and young people on the path to success. The indicators of this PSA highlight our priorities for action over the next three years and beyond:

- increase participation in positive activities;

- reduce the proportion of young people frequently using illicit drugs, alcohol or volatile substances;

- reduce the under-18 conception rate;

- reduce the number of first-time entrants to the criminal justice system aged 10–17; and

- reduce the number of 16–18-year-olds not in education, employment or training (NEET).

6.8 The significant progress we have already made is a tribute to young people themselves, their parents, and to those in the children's workforce who support them. As set out in *Children and Young People Today*, contrary to some perceptions, most young people are achieving more than previous generations and playing a greater role in our communities than ever before. We have also made significant progress in tackling entrenched problems that have a serious impact on wider society, and put young people's own futures at risk. For example, rates of teenage pregnancy are at their lowest for 20 years and illicit drug use among young people fell between 1998 and 2004/05.

6.9 We also signalled in *Aiming High for Young People* that enabling all young people to navigate successfully the increasingly complex and changing environment in which they grow up requires a new approach that focuses on building their resilience and affirms their place in society. The success of this approach depends on schools, colleges, services, communities and parents working together to ensure that young people succeed in and out of learning no matter what obstacles they face. To support this, we are setting a goal that by 2020 **all young people will be participating in positive activities to develop personal and social skills, to promote their wellbeing and to reduce the behaviour that puts young people at risk.**

6.10 While our priority is to provide all young people with opportunities and support, we must accompany this with greater progress in breaking down barriers and securing better futures for young people who are most at risk. There continues to be young people who sometimes remain beyond the reach of services, who do poorly in learning, and who are alienated from their communities. We know that these young people often experience multiple, overlapping problems and risks:

- persistent truants are nearly ten times more likely to be NEET at 16 and four times more likely to be NEET at 18;

- young people with emotional and behavioural difficulties are four times more likely to use illicit drugs;

- three in five excluded young people report having offended; and

- 71 per cent of young women who are NEET for six months or more between 16–18 years of age are parents by 21.

6.11 The reasons why some are still left behind are complex and not always predictable. But there are common causes:

- lack of support from their families;

- experiencing poverty in the home;

- living in neighbourhoods affected by crime and deprivation; and

- experiencing poor public services and lack of opportunities.

6.12 The extent and density of these multiple and overlapping problems explains in part why some young people get involved in crime. Tackling crime is a measure of how effectively we are preventing a wider range of problems and improving outcomes for the most disaffected young people.

6.13 We must also recognise that there are new pressures that affect young people today that will potentially increase these problems if left unchecked. We know that while opportunities have increased so too have some risks. And there are some issues, such as heavier alcohol consumption by some young people, where there is a need for a more ambitious approach.

6.14 Success will only be achieved by addressing all of the issues facing these teenagers. It depends on everyone – parents, families, schools and colleges, government, local services, communities and employers – having high aspirations for young people and working closely with young people themselves to join up more effectively and deliver better services, focusing on prevention and early intervention, to bring about the long-term improvements that are needed.

Key areas for reform

6.15 We are already working with local authorities and other key partners to transform young people's services. The Children's Plan builds on recent reforms in six areas where young people, their parents and those who support them say we need to do better:

- provision of better **support for parents and families** coping with challenging behaviour by their children;

- provision of **universal opportunities for positive activities**, achieving major improvements in things for all young people to do in their areas and places for them to go;

- improvements in **the local delivery** of high quality services for young people, focusing on the faster integration of services for the most vulnerable and a renewed focus on early intervention and prevention to stop problems becoming entrenched;

- stronger action to **tackle behaviour that puts young people at risk** – in particular in relation to alcohol consumption, where new evidence suggests the need for a more ambitious approach, and substance misuse;

- helping to create **more cohesive and resilient communities**, where young people feel confident in interacting with others and where diversity and difference is valued rather than feared; and

- more effective action by children's services and youth justice agencies to **reduce youth crime** through a reformed approach to youth justice, that has a stronger emphasis on prevention, rehabilitation and action to stop repeat offences by young people.

6.16 Important also to these reforms is the provision of high quality, impartial and seamless information, advice and guidance to help young people understand their options and make decisions. Further details are set out in Chapter 5.

Support for parents and families

6.17 Evidence shows that parents remain the most direct influence on young people's outcomes, shaping their aspirations and values. We need to work with parents to help ensure that young people benefit from this influence, so that the problems that some parents face are not passed on to young people.

6.18 Some parents struggle to manage their children's behaviour or experience other difficulties that affect their ability to provide good guidance and support. There is a lack of targeted parenting support for groups whom we know might benefit, such as parents who are offenders, prisoners, or drug users. We need to do more to help parents manage challenging behaviour and we will bring forward proposals to this end. We will expand parenting support available through extended schools. And we will develop proposals for a number of local authorities to further develop targeted parenting support.

6.19 We will also increase the number of local parenting support teams building on the 77 Respect parenting experts already in place. The teams will comprise up to four experts working through extended schools and across the local authority, supporting parents who most need help to manage their children's behaviour. The local parenting strategy will guide how their support is targeted, and they will also assist the commissioner for parenting support in targeting existing activity. They will also provide expertise which could be used to support the development of parent-peer support teams based on the 'expert patient' model.

Places to go, things to do

6.20 *Aiming high for young people: A ten year strategy for positive activities* sets out our ambition to transform the opportunities for young people in their leisure time and give them an equal place in communities. It explains the importance of high quality activities in helping young people develop broader skills, including resilience, and have higher ambitions.

6.21 The challenge is for local services to deliver this strategy in a way that involves and empowers all young people, removes barriers to access, and, crucially, increases the quality of what is on offer locally. We start from a good position – through the Youth Opportunity and Capital Funds we have placed real power and influence in the hands of young people with over half a million teenagers benefiting. And we have ensured that there are clear accountabilities on local authorities to address the lack of priority in this area in the past.

6.22 We now need to turn this strategy into real improvement on the ground. We will publish an implementation plan early next year that sets out the roles of government, local authorities, third and private sector providers, and schools and colleges in delivering *Aiming high for young people*.

6.23 There are three areas where we want to strengthen the commitments made in *Aiming high*:

- setting a clear goal that all young people will participate in positive activities and access a broad range of experiences;
- making further investment to provide places to go in every community; and
- exploring ways of improving further information about things to do and places to go.

Increasing participation in positive activities

6.24 Many young people already take part in and enjoy a range of positive experiences. But too often disadvantaged young people do not have the same opportunity as their peers. The cost might be prohibitive, or availability limited, access difficult, or they may simply think it is 'not for them'. We want all young people to participate in a range of positive activities that broadens their experience and develops their interests and talent. Our *Aiming high* strategy and implementation plan will drive agreement between central and local government on delivery priorities. It will support our aims of empowering local communities, allowing young people to hold government and local services to account for its effective delivery.

6.25   In driving progress towards our goal of all young people participating in positive activities, local authorities and their partners will focus on ensuring that all young people make use of the opportunities available to them, and also that the quarter of young people who do not currently participate are given sufficient priority – including disabled young people who can face additional barriers to accessing this provision.

6.26   As corporate parents, local authorities should consider how to improve access to positive activities for children in care, including free access to their leisure facilities. Following the Children and Young Persons Bill, we will set out how participation in positive leisure activities should form part of the care plan for all children and young people in care.

6.27   Some children said to us in the *Time to Talk* video diaries that they are not given enough opportunities to get involved in the things they might enjoy, like sport and music, and children feel that they miss out if they or their families cannot afford these activities. All young people should have a full range of experiences throughout the teenage years. **We believe that going further in defining an entitlement will give young people higher and clearer expectations.** We will consult young people on what range of experiences could be part of this entitlement.

6.28   As well as sport, central to this entitlement will be participation in cultural activity, which enriches lives and contributes to all five of the Every Child Matters outcomes. We recently announced a major school music programme and will now go further. **We will work towards a position where no matter where they live, or what their background, all children and young people have the opportunities to get involved in top quality cultural opportunities in and out of school.** We will work towards a five hour offer to match that for sport. The aim will be to give young people the chance to develop as:

●   informed spectators (through attending top quality theatre and dance performances, world class exhibitions, galleries, museums and heritage sites); and

●   participants and creators (through learning a musical instrument, playing and singing in ensembles, taking part in theatre and dance performances, producing an artwork, making films and media art, or curating an exhibition).

6.29   We will mount a series of pilots looking at different approaches in different parts of the country, and establish a Youth Culture Trust to run these and promote cultural activities more widely. There will be an emphasis on young people working with the very best of the professional cultural sector. Where young people show particular talents in an area we will ensure that they have the opportunities to develop this and, where appropriate, progress into careers in the cultural and creative industries.

A place to go in every community

6.30   As *Aiming high* described we are clear about the importance of attractive safe facilities for young people in every community providing high quality youth clubs and activity groups, run by inspirational workers and volunteers. It also set out the role of local authorities in taking a more strategic approach to using all available assets to deliver this. Through the ongoing implementation of extended provision we are also increasing access to activities through school.

6.31 We have already committed £60 million to start transforming youth facilities and identified that young people's services will be a priority for the unclaimed assets fund. **In addition, we will invest a further £160 million in the first two years,** prior to the unclaimed assets money becoming available. Unclaimed assets funding remains fully additional to this provision. We will make sure that all projects are built on effective partnerships with local authorities, the third and private sectors as well as involving young people in decision making so that the transformation of facilities takes account of their ideas about what they will need and use. We have identified the BIG Lottery Fund as the preferred delivery agent for both government and unclaimed assets funding, although they will be accounted for separately.

Better information

6.32 The *Time to Talk* consultation with young people showed that lack of good information about what is available remains a barrier to participating in positive activities.

6.33 Local authorities have a duty to publicise information about activities, and have been provided with funds to support this. But we know that some would benefit from more support in both mapping the information about what is available, and getting the information to young people.

6.34 **We will explore opportunities for further investment in supporting local authorities to improve the information available to young people and their families.** This will involve the use of new technologies and 'formats' that young people use on a daily basis such as social networking and viral marketing, including enabling them to generate and share their own information and views about provision.

6.35 As a first step we will engage with commercial providers of ICT, communications and internet services to determine their interest in working with government and local authorities to transform the quality of information.

Case study for positive activities: Sunderland

Sunderland established a Youth Board in 2007 that ensures that the City has a range of innovative programmes and activities for young people, high quality support and guidance, and a range of volunteering opportunities – delivering a co-ordinated and coherent youth offer.

The Youth Opportunity Fund and Youth Capital Fund (YCF) have funded 12 successful youth-led projects that have been set up to improve and develop youth provision in some areas where it was lacking. This has resulted in a wide range of participation from children of all backgrounds, including disadvantaged and hard to reach groups of young people, including young carers, homeless young people, young offenders and black and minority ethnic young people. These have involved 103 young people, leading and managing projects that will benefit over 3,000 young people.

Young Asian Voices (YAV) received £25,000 of YCF funding to establish a base for the black and minority ethnic young people in Sunderland. This will give young people the opportunity to meet and learn from other young people from different backgrounds. YAV will work in association with other organisations, and local people in a common effort to advance education, health, welfare, training, leisure and employment opportunities that improve their social economic life chances.

In March 2007 Sunderland won the Communities and Local Government Digital Challenge, bringing £5 million of investment to the City. The competition was aimed at finding the best use of IT to connect with the community. One of the reasons that Sunderland won was the fact that the ICT function has an e-neighbourhood team focused entirely on the needs of the community, delivering Electronic Village Halls and supporting an e-champion network. This approach has also resulted in Sunderland delivering the Empowering Young People Pilot (EYPP) which is due to begin early in 2008. This will test new ways of giving young people more direct choice and spending power in accessing positive activities. A wide range of activities are offered through up to 100 private, public and voluntary organisations.

Effective delivery in every local area

6.36 A pressing challenge is to strengthen delivery of policies in local areas to ensure that young people receive the support they need, when they need it, in a way which enables it to have the most effect.

6.37 While we are seeing real progress in some areas, historic problems remain which restrict effective delivery in every area:

- young people can still experience unco-ordinated interventions or fall through the gaps in service provision – caused by lack of integrated strategy, management, and front line practice;

- some services are not available or lack investment and crucial elements of support are often missing because of this;

- there is sometimes a poor understanding about the respective roles of schools and targeted services in providing better support; and

- the capacity of the workforce is under-developed in some areas.

6.38 **We have therefore established a new Youth Task Force** as a streamlined driver for improved delivery. It will publish an action plan in the spring setting out how it will improve delivery on young people's issues, working with local areas and regional partners to provide support and build improvement capacity. This will include doing more to bring together the work of field forces on these issues at a local level.

6.39 One early priority for the Youth Task Force will be to work with local authorities and other key partners to drive improvements in support for vulnerable young people, achievement of which underpins a number of our delivery priorities.

6.40 By the end of 2008 we want every area to have arrangements in place across all their services, including schools, children's services and health and youth justice services, for early identification of vulnerable young people, prevention of problems before they escalate, and joined up support coordinated by a lead professional when problems do emerge.

6.41 In order to ensure the effective delivery of policies for young people in every local area we will:

- design and establish stronger and more integrated delivery arrangements to support the Targeted Youth Support reforms and delivery of the new young people PSA, at local level and regional level, incorporating greater delivery expertise in frontline practice with vulnerable teenagers;

- examine the need for a youth delivery framework for local authorities – a combined tool for all the young people PSA outcomes, that local authorities can use to be clear what good delivery involves, that helps them identify their local challenges and draw on tailored delivery support to tackle them. We will investigate whether greater evidence-based consistency in the delivery of targeted support would accelerate delivery and impact on young people's outcomes; and

- explore how web-based tools could be used to broaden access to support, and – by enabling young people to identify their own needs, and by making initial steps to support easier and less threatening to them – help young people to come forward for support earlier than they otherwise might.

6.42 Extended schools are important to meeting the needs and aspirations of teenagers in their communities. Extended schools will offer a range of out of school activities for young people, as well as increasingly opening up school facilities for wider community use, bringing the community into schools. Extended schools, working closely with local youth support services, will support prevention and provide swift and easy access to targeted support where necessary.

6.43 In addition, to ensure that we have a skilled and competent workforce delivering across the country, the Government will invest £25 million over the next three years to reform the youth workforce, as set out in *Aiming high*. This will address four main areas: leadership and management, recruitment and retention, building third sector capacity, and introducing a

Tackling behaviour that puts young people at risk

6.44 The offer of positive activities, together with the reforms to 14–19 learning set out in Chapter 5, is designed to provide an attractive universal offer to young people in and out of learning so that they can make a successful transition to adulthood.

6.45 But these reforms must be complemented by stronger action to reduce the risks that face young people, build resilience and then intervene early when they make bad decisions and start getting into trouble.

Reducing alcohol consumption

6.46 We know that the proportion of young people drinking alcohol is falling. However, the level of consumption amongst those young people who *do* drink doubled in the ten years to 2000 and has remained at the same level since. Consuming too much alcohol at a young age can harm young people's health as well as contributing to a wide range of other problems such as teenage pregnancy, offending, and becoming a victim of crime and drug use.

6.47 The Government's updated alcohol harm reduction strategy – *Safe, Sensible, Social* – identifies for the first time under-18s as a priority group for government action on alcohol. Current actions include renewing efforts to reduce underage sales, delivering a social marketing campaign to change attitudes towards young people's drinking, and setting up a panel of experts who will develop guidance for young people and their parents on the specific health harms associated with young people's alcohol consumption.

6.48 We will build on this to address heavy 'binge' drinking by young people by working with children's services, schools and parents so young people who are experiencing substance misuse problems receive appropriate interventions from the right agencies at the right time. Schools can play an important role. We will help schools and children's services to be more alert to problems of alcohol misuse and to make sure that the workforce is equipped to respond appropriately and involve relevant agencies when necessary.

6.49 Schools are also in a good position to communicate the right messages and spot alcohol misuse problems early. Alcohol education in schools must be accurate and effective. We will examine the effectiveness of current delivery arrangements for all drugs education – including alcohol – and act to strengthen them if necessary.

6.50 We will take more action on parental alcohol misuse, which can put children and young people at risk, as well as having a negative influence on young people's own drinking patterns. There are three initiatives which will help us in our drive to address problems of parental alcohol misuse:

- Family Pathfinders, which will commence in April 2008, will bring together children's and adult services to ensure that families with complex needs receive a whole family package of support;

- Family Intervention Projects, which work with some of the most challenging families, will be expanded to offer support in 58 local authority areas across the country; and

- in 77 areas, parenting practitioners will offer support to parents experiencing difficulties.

6.51 We will review the effectiveness of these initiatives for reaching and supporting alcohol misusing parents and, working with key stakeholders such as the National Academy for Parenting Practitioners, we will strengthen our approach if necessary.

6.52 Next year, as part of a youth alcohol action plan, we will look carefully at what more the Government can do, using all the levers at our disposal to impact upon young people's alcohol consumption. We will:

- explore how we can place alcohol further from the reach of young people by tackling **low price sales** of alcohol;

- explore what more we could do to **deter young people from attempting to buy** alcohol and, if they do, how we can intensify confiscation efforts;

- in the context of the existing review of alcohol price, promotion and harm, consider the case for further action to protect children and young people from **alcohol advertising**;

- explore how we might prevent young people **drinking alcohol in public places** where they are unsupervised, as we know that the risk of harm increases in these circumstances; and

- work with our partners to strengthen our **evidence base** on young people and alcohol.

Reducing the use of drugs

6.53 We know that the use of drugs by young people is falling. However, levels of illicit drug use are still relatively high compared to the rest of Europe. As with alcohol, the evidence is clear that young people's drug use contributes to a wide range of other serious problems experienced by teenagers, such as failing or falling behind at school, involvement in crime and anti-social behaviour, mental health problems, as well as risks of overdose and future drug dependency.

6.54 The Government's current approach to young people and drugs is driven through the cross-departmental ten year national drug strategy, which comes to an end in March 2008 and is currently being reviewed. This approach has focused on interventions with young people who are starting to misuse drugs or at risk of doing so, and on aligning local action on drugs by Drug Action Teams and children's services.

6.55 The existing strategy has contributed to a fall in the proportion of all young people using drugs, a 17 per cent reduction between 2003 and 2006 in the numbers of vulnerable young people frequently using illicit drugs, and to better identification and referral to treatment of young people who need additional help. We also have exceeded our target to increase numbers of young people in treatment by 50 per cent a year early, rising from 6,530 in 2003/04 to 21,765 in 2006/07. Drug education in schools is improving and the cross-departmental awareness campaign FRANK has become a trusted source of information and guidance to young people and their parents.

6.56 Building on this progress, we know that more is needed to:

- tackle drug misuse by parents, which can put children and young people at risk of significant harm. We need to do more to ensure that substance misuse within families is being identified and that appropriate support is offered early;

- improve the quality and coverage of specialist drug treatment for the young people who experience the most serious harm from drugs, building on progress to date; and

- strengthen and clarify the role of both schools and children's services in drug, alcohol and volatile substance misuse prevention, taking account in particular of the comprehensive study of the impact of drugs education in schools, (the Blueprint study) expected early next year, and looking at what more we need to do to support schools in dealing with pupils who are misusing substances.

6.57 We will address these issues through **next year's revised cross-government drugs strategy**, in which young people and families will be a key priority.

Improving young people's sexual health

6.58 The Expert Group debates included discussions on the development of good relationships, healthy behavioural and emotional development and its importance as children develop through adolescence into adults. We recognise that many young people feel that they do not currently have the knowledge they need to make safe and responsible choices in relation to their sexual health. **We will therefore review best practice in effective sex and relationships education and how it is delivered in schools**, involving young people fully to ensure it better meets their needs. We will also increase young people's knowledge of effective contraception and improve their access to advice through encouraging the provision of on-site health services in schools, colleges and youth centres.

> *"Ensure that teachers who teach sex education in schools have adequate training to deliver young people's entitlement to SRE. We believe that there needs to be a greater emphasis on the number of teachers and school nurses who receive the specialist training."*
> (Practitioner, Time to Talk consultation)

Cohesive and resilient communities

6.59 Young people today are growing up increasingly exposed to global influences and within an increasingly diverse society in the UK. This brings huge opportunities but it can also bring uncertainties. For example, young people may feel they have competing identities and be uncertain of their place in their local community and in wider British society. This can be a barrier to young people achieving their potential. It can also lead to tension and concern in local communities, and leave young people vulnerable to being influenced by those who seek to exaggerate and exploit diversity and difference, including by encouraging the use of violence or other criminal behaviour.

6.60 Young people are also concerned about their relentlessly negative image. This can create suspicion and divisions in communities, especially between young people and older people.

6.61 We must all work together to create more cohesive, safer communities, helping young people to develop a sense of belonging and appreciation of those from other cultures and backgrounds. We must also promote the mutual benefits of communication, contact and joint enterprise between younger and older people. Young people are citizens too and the majority want to exercise their responsibilities positively and have their contributions to their communities acknowledged.

6.62 The new duty on schools to promote community cohesion recognises the central role schools can play, and through the *Aiming high* strategy we will encourage positive activities that give young people from different backgrounds the opportunity to come together outside school.

6.63 The Government is also committed to working alongside local communities and those working with young people to build resilience to the specific threat from violent extremist groups who seek to undermine the values that we all share. Increased political awareness is a normal part of growing up and we should encourage young people to express their views. But young people need to understand that the use of violence in any context, including to further a cause, whether it is the rights of animals or particular political or ideological views, is criminal.

6.64 Local authorities are already funding a number of community-based projects working with young people and **an additional £45 million has been announced for building resilience at a community level over the next three years. We will consult young people including through a new youth panel on how best to support them in rejecting extremism.** And we will set up a headteachers' forum to consult schools on what further help they need to raise awareness of the risks of violent extremism, encourage open discussion and debate about controversial issues, and work in effective local partnerships to support vulnerable young people.

Reducing youth crime

6.65 The significant majority of young people do not offend. And most of those that do offend do not commit serious offences. Around half of youth crime is committed by a small minority of prolific offenders. Overall levels of youth crime and of all offence types remained broadly stable between 2003 and 2005. We need to respond to the concerns of communities and young people themselves about crime to secure a significant fall over time in the proportion of young people who offend.

6.66 Children told us in the *Time to Talk* video diaries how they want to feel safe in the areas they live in and feel that crime needs to be reduced.

6.67 Youth crime affects young people themselves. Most crime committed against young people is perpetrated by other young people. Young victims and offenders can be the same people subject to the same problems and risk factors. We need to improve our systems for supporting young victims of crime. For example, young victims are concerned that they will not be listened to if they report a crime, or that they will be labelled a 'grass'. Others simply do not know how to report a crime. We need to improve young people's confidence in the whole criminal justice system. And we need to understand better why some young victims go on to become offenders, and how to prevent this happening.

6.68 The new cross-government responsibilities for youth justice present an opportunity to look at how we might strengthen the approach we are taking to offending by young people. We know that key to reducing youth crime is the engagement of mainstream services as well as making the best use of targeted interventions. This is important whether in prevention, information sharing and safeguarding, during community sentences and custody and in resettlement as young people move out of formal involvement with the youth justice system. We must build on existing good practice of partnership working to ensure continuity of provision for all young people in contact with the criminal justice system.

6.69 So we are taking a fundamental look at the way in which the criminal justice system overall is working for young people to ensure we learn from existing good practice and address current concerns. This includes examining what we know about why young people offend, what a more effective approach to prevention would look like, the options available for dealing with children who commit crimes, how we can use the time when young people are in contact with the criminal justice system to reduce re-offending and how best to tackle the most serious offenders. Detailed action on how we will jointly tackle these problems will be set out in next year's Youth Crime Action Plan. We aim **to significantly reduce by 2020 the number of young people receiving a conviction, reprimand or final warning for a recordable offence for the first time, with a goal to be set in the Youth Crime Action Plan**.

Crime prevention

6.70 We know that those who become prolific offenders face a number of challenges at home and in the community and will need support long before offending behaviour emerges. The signals are often clear, and it is never too early to intervene. We must put in place responsive high quality universal services with greater support for those who need it most, including tackling anti-social behaviour.

6.71 We are encouraging headteachers and Chief Constables to consider the places where Safer Schools Partnerships might be established. Safer Schools Partnerships help reduce youth crime through supporting a police presence on school premises, and should be extended to a wider range of schools.

6.72 We will do more to tackle anti-social behaviour by giving the young people involved more support to help them address the problems behind their poor behaviour, alongside enforcement measures to reduce the frequency of anti-social behaviour and progression to more serious criminal activity.

6.73 The Youth Task Force will work with a number of local authorities around the country to establish the most effective way to ensure that enforcement activity comes with greater support for young people, especially those who are clearly at risk of developing further problems, where our ambition is to intervene early to prevent problems spiralling. In doing so, we will work with the Youth Justice Board and other national and local partners already working with children and young people most at risk of getting involved in anti-social behaviour or low level crime and disorder, building on recognised tiered approaches of identification, assessment, preventive activity and intervention. In particular the Task Force will:

- run a **pilot in 47 areas where local authorities will be encouraged to accompany all applications for Anti-Social Behaviour orders with an Individual Support Order or appropriate support.** Individual Support Orders ensure that appropriate support is provided to a young person who is in receipt of an anti-social behaviour order to address the underlying causes of anti-social behaviour. They have been shown to reduce the risk of re-offending for young people; and

- work with local authorities to help them adopt an approach already used in some areas, where young people are systematically offered support whenever enforcement activity (for example warning letter, then Acceptable Behaviour Contracts) is needed. This should help prevent them progressing onto more serious problem behaviour which requires measures like anti-social behaviour orders or criminal sanctions.

6.74 In the longer term, in addition to Targeted Youth Support reforms referred to previously in this chapter, we will:

- consolidate our evidence on what interventions with young people and their families make the most difference to preventing young people's involvement in crime so as to spread best practice;

- continue to develop and adopt best practice across Government to work with local partners including schools, children's services, the police, the third sector and Youth Offending Teams, to focus on the young people and families most at risk of involvement in crime and to ensure the necessary interventions are happening early enough; and

- achieve greater alignment between children's services and the youth justice system, including where necessary pooling budgets to increase reach and impact.

Consequences for young offenders

6.75 Young people must take responsibility for their actions, and those who commit crimes must be held to account and dealt with appropriately, with a range of options for tackling low level offences through to custodial sentences for the minority of young offenders who commit the most serious offences. But we also know that the likelihood of re-offending increases the further a young person gets into the criminal justice system.

6.76 We must reduce recidivism by promoting rehabilitation and by treating first time offences, particularly minor ones, appropriately so that young people do not receive a disproportionately harsh response for low level offences. It is important we have a system with a complementary menu of options to meet the individual young person's needs and tackle their particular situation and level of offending. This includes being able to deal appropriately with particularly low level offences.

6.77 **We intend therefore to pilot a restorative approach to youth offenders from April 2008.** The Youth Restorative Disposal aims to prevent re-offending through a more rehabilitative approach and the involvement of victims so offenders have to face up to the consequences of even low level offending, and the pilots will look at whether this is a more appropriate way to deal with particularly low level, first offences.

6.78 We also need to look at the existing range of options, both before and in court, to ensure that practitioners have a clear framework that allows for both rigour and flexibility. They and the courts must be able to focus their attention where it is most needed. This is why the Government is taking forward legislation in the Criminal Justice and Immigration Bill to introduce the Youth Rehabilitation Order. This will provide the courts with a flexible community order with a range of requirements that can be tailored to meet the individual young person's needs and offending behaviour.

6.79 We also need to build on effective partnership working between the Youth Offending Teams and children's services to reduce risk factors associated with re-offending as part of our reforms of targeted youth support services. There is also an important role for the community and we will look at how to increase their involvement, for example through extending referral panels.

6.80 **Therefore for the Youth Crime Action Plan we will look at the overall way we treat children in the criminal justice system, with a focus on the treatment of 10–15-year-olds to ensure we are meeting this younger age group's particular needs. This will include examining the approaches other countries use to reduce offending amongst young people.**

Reforms to the secure estate

6.81 For some young offenders custody will be right and necessary and we must continue to build on existing work to ensure it is run by committed, well-trained staff, with dedicated facilities. But we also need to explore the alternatives to custody, such as intensive fostering. Similarly, we will look at the configuration of the juvenile secure estate to explore whether there would be benefits in alternative settings with stronger links to the community to aid resettlement.

6.82 We must ensure rigorous safeguarding for those young people in custodial settings. The Youth Justice Board's strategy for the secure estate sets out measures that include well developed self harm, suicide and bullying prevention programmes, measures to prevent harm from adults and provision of independent advocacy services. But we must be constantly looking at whether more is needed. This is why on 26 July, David Hanson, the Minister for Youth Justice and Beverley Hughes, the Minister for Children, Young People and Families, announced a joint review by Andrew Williamson and Peter Smallridge, of the use of restraint on juveniles in secure training centres, secure children's homes and young offender institutions. Among the issues which the review is looking at are the operational efficacy, medical safety and ethical validity of restraint methods. This is an important and sensitive subject. The review, which is being independently chaired, is currently consulting with a wide range of stakeholders before reporting to Ministers in April 2008.

6.83 We need to maximise the use of the time when young people are in contact with the criminal justice system to tackle offending behaviour and underlying causes. It is important that all young offenders, whether in the community or in custody are able to access the full range of services they need. This includes improving the education of young offenders to better reflect the experience of their peers in mainstream education. All young offenders should receive education and training which is based on that in mainstream schools and colleges, but which recognises the additional education support and wider needs they often have. We must ensure that young people in the youth justice system receive a consistent education and training experience, in which they can progress and achieve. It must support them to fulfil their potential and to continue and progress into further training and employment.

6.84 **We will publish a Green Paper in 2008 exploring how we can improve post-justice continuity of care.** We want to examine how we can improve the services young people receive once they leave custody or the supervision of a Youth Offending Team. The Green Paper will cover wider proposals for how we improve education for young offenders, in custody and the community, including plans linking offender education more strongly with the 14–19 curriculum, quality improvement and workforce development, and access and participation in education for young offenders in the community. It will also look at the support other services provide to ensure that these young people are given the best chance to move forward and reduce the risk of re-offending. This will include examining what we can learn from the support offered to young people leaving care. We will also consult early in 2008 on our intention to place a duty on local authorities to make them responsible for a young person's education while they are in custody (in line with mainstream education responsibilities of local authorities). We will do this in line with the reforms set out in Chapter 5 for 14–19 education.

Conclusion

6.85 This chapter has set out the actions we will take to ensure that those young people who encounter, or are at risk of encountering, problems which will restrict their ability to reach their full potential, are helped to stay on, or get back on, the path to success. Together with the other reforms set out in the Children's Plan, they will help to ensure that as many young people as possible have a childhood and a transition to adulthood which enables them to reach their potential and have fulfilling, economically and socially successful lives.

Chapter 7: Making it happen

Vision for 21st century children's services

Executive summary

7.1   Delivering the vision set out in the Children's Plan will require a series of system-wide reforms to the way services for children and young people work together. By putting the needs of children and families first, we will provide a service that makes more sense to the parents, children and young people using them, for whom professional boundaries can appear arbitrary and frustrating. By locating services under one roof in the places people visit frequently, they are more likely to find the help they need. And by investing in all of those who work with children, and by building capacity to work across professional boundaries, we can ensure that joining up services is not just about providing a safety net for the vulnerable – it is about unlocking the potential of every child.

7.2   We want to build on the ambitions set out in Every Child Matters, and deliver a step change in outcomes. We will:

- expect every school to be uncompromising in its ambitions for achievement, sitting at the heart of the community it serves;

- set high expectations for Children's Trusts to:
  - deliver measurable improvements for all children and young people;
  - have in place by 2010 consistent, high quality arrangements to provide identification and early intervention for all children and young people who need additional help;

- monitor the difference Children's Trusts are making and examine whether Children's Trust arrangements need to be strengthened to improve outcomes, including by further legislation; and

- publish a Children's Workforce Action Plan in early 2008, covering everyone who works with children and young people, which will strengthen integrated working across all services.

Introduction

7.3   Delivering the goals we have set out in the preceding chapters will require a series of system-wide reforms to the way services for children and young people work together.

7.4   In Every Child Matters, we set out an ambition that services should work together to ensure every child can be healthy, stay safe, enjoy and achieve, make a positive contribution and achieve economic wellbeing. However, despite the reforms to join up children's services at a local level, we haven't always been consistent in our message about how important it is that services work together, not just to provide a safety net for the vulnerable, but to unlock the potential of every child. A focus on ensuring children are healthy will not work without considering their participation in activities which can help them stay healthy. Children cannot achieve at school if they do not feel safe at home or outside. Poverty will blight our attempts to ensure children can enjoy school.

7.5 Together we want to build a system that provides opportunity and delivers services to meet the needs of children and young people, supports parents and carers, and intervenes early where additional support is needed to get a child or young person back onto the path to success. These services need to be delivered by skilled and motivated staff, who achieve excellence in their specialism and work to a shared ambition for the success of every child.

7.6 Some have argued that if we focus on the range of outcomes that make up a good childhood, we will compromise our capacity to deliver on any one. As this plan demonstrates, the opposite is true. Attainment is the biggest single predictor of a successful adult life, but a successful education is not a product simply of what happens in schools and colleges. As our experts and the parents and children we asked told us, we can only succeed by looking at all aspects of a child's life in the round.

7.7 By working around the needs of the child, we will also provide services that make more sense to those using them. Distinctions and boundaries that mean something to professionals can appear arbitrary and frustrating to the parent or child in need of help. And by co-locating services in the places parents, children and young people routinely use we make life much more convenient, and increase the chances that people will find the help they need.

Universal services in a preventative system

7.8 Almost all children, young people and families come into regular contact with early years settings and with schools and colleges. That means early years settings, schools and colleges must sit at the heart of an effective system of prevention and early intervention working in partnership with parents and families. They are the places where children and young people build the breadth of experience that makes for a rounded childhood. If these services are not integrated with more specialist provision, by looking for early warnings that children might need more help and by providing facilities for specialist services to operate so they can be easily reached by children and families, we will be hamstrung in achieving our broad ambitions for children and young people. The best schools and colleges have already shown us how that can be done and that it enhances, not compromises, attainment.

7.9 Different local authorities, schools, colleges or other services are at different stages in developing a fully integrated system designed around the needs of children and families. Some areas have made great strides in building integrated working and shared objectives across services. In other areas there are pockets of good practice. Some places still have a long way to go.

7.10 Different areas face different problems, and arrangements that work in one place are not necessarily appropriate elsewhere. There is no single approach. But in the Children's Plan we want to be clear about the high expectations we have that Children's Trusts, under local authority leadership, will deliver better outcomes for children and young people in all aspects of their lives and will bring services together to do so.

7.11 The Children's Plan sets out some important steps to build capacity and capability, strengthen incentives and sharpen accountability so that we have a system in place that will deliver our ambitions for 2020. For example:

- 0–7 partnerships will enable early years providers, health services and primary schools to work together to provide a more seamless local service for children and parents; and

- 14–19 partnerships will bring together schools, colleges and other providers, with employers and guidance services, to deliver new entitlements to young people. Through working together, they will offer more to young people than any one of them could offer by acting alone. Between them they will offer entitlements to all the new Diplomas, together with the full range of other curriculum and qualification opportunities. The partnerships will be one of the most significant reshapings of the education system of recent years.

Box 7.1 – The 21st century school

Schools play a central role in helping children achieve their potential and enjoy their childhood. A school's distinctive contribution is in excellent teaching and learning, ensuring children achieve. But schools are also places where children develop confidence, self-respect and respect for others, learn about teamwork and leadership, and about responsibility and successful relationships.

Schools are a vital community resource. Almost all children and young people spend time in school, both during the school day and outside it. Most families trust and are familiar with their school, and schools are also accessible to the wider community. Schools can therefore offer wider opportunities for children, young people and their families to take part in sport or cultural activities as well as learning.

Because schools know their pupils well, and understand what opportunities they need and what may prevent them from succeeding, they are places where emerging problems can be identified and addressed early and swiftly, either by the school itself or by engaging specialist help.

The **21st century school** is a school that excels in each of these dimensions. It provides an excellent education and by personalising learning does not compromise in its mission to see each child achieve all of which he or she is capable. But it also actively contributes to all aspects of a child's life – health and wellbeing, safety, and developing the wider experiences and skills that characterise a good childhood and set a young person up for success as an adult. It contributes to these wider areas because they help children achieve, but also because they are good for children's wider development and part of a good childhood.

The school actively engages and listens to parents, makes sure their views shape school policies, and works with them as partners in their child's learning and development.

It looks beyond the pupils on its roll, and works in partnership with other schools to ensure education in the local area is as good as it can be. It plays a central role in the wider community, opening its facilities for the benefit of families and others, and is conscious of its role in a sustainable society.

Every child should have a personal tutor, someone in the school who knows them well, helps them to identify and plan to meet their ambitions and to act quickly if problems emerge, talking to parents and bringing in other support where necessary.

The 21st century school can only fulfil its potential if it can rely on other, often specialist, services for children being there when needed – including health (for example mental health and speech and language therapy), early years and childcare, behaviour, youth, and crime prevention services. It needs to be an active partner in planning and delivery arrangements under Children's Trusts, helping to define the priorities for their local area, and agreeing how the whole pattern of local services best fits together to meet need.

If we are to achieve our 2020 goals for children and young people, every school will need to realise this vision of a 21st century school.

Box 7.2 – Co-location of services

Bringing different services together in places that children, young people and families visit often offers a number of advantages:

- a **one-stop shop** is convenient and avoids stigma. The evidence shows that they make it more likely that children, young people and families who need them will use services which they might not otherwise think of visiting;

- staff in co-located services are more likely to talk to each other and provide **joined-up support**. For example, co-location of health visitors and midwives helps smooth transition between antenatal and postnatal periods;

- informal day-to-day contact can help staff better communicate, build trusting relationships and adopt more **co-operative working practices**;

- co-location provides opportunities for joint planning and making the most out of existing **resources** such as staff, equipment, rooms and other facilities; and

- co-location can help build strong links with local communities, helping services to be more **responsive to local needs**.

7.12 We have already put in place the means to make collaboration work in practice following the Children Act 2004, the Education Act 2005, the Education and Inspections Act 2006 and the Childcare Act 2006. We have seen good practice develop on the ground and we need to build on this foundation to strengthen Children's Trust arrangements, ensuring they deliver high quality in all areas rather than just partnership for its own sake.

Children's Trusts to drive collaboration

7.13 Making a reality of the vision for our children set out the Children's Plan depends on parents, the community, statutory services, the voluntary sector and business working together to provide opportunities, tackle problems and transform the environment in which children grow up.

7.14 At local level, the lead lies with local authorities, working with other partners as Children's Trusts. The 2004 Children Act put one person in charge locally, the Director of Children's Services (DCS). We look to the DCS working with their elected counterpart, the Lead Member for Children, to bring together all relevant local agencies and wider interests as a strong and dynamic Children's Trust.

7.15 The Children's Trust is a broad coalition of all those interested locally in the wellbeing of children. NHS services, particularly local Primary Care Trusts, are members of this coalition, as are the police. We expect all key local authority services, at district as well as at top tier level in two tier authorities, including those such as housing, transport, planning and leisure whose focus is not exclusively on children, and local authority and other agencies concerned with economic prosperity, skills and regeneration, to play their part.

Box 7.3 – Local authorities leading the system

Local authorities are uniquely placed to champion the needs of local communities, to take a strategic view across a range of services and to prioritise spending where it will have the biggest impact. They alone have the mandate and broad local knowledge to shape supply and demand, and to drive change through Children's Trust partnership arrangements. This requires strong local leadership from councillors, making tough choices and ensuring that the needs of the user are always paramount. Services, including schools, must be commissioned in a way that is tailored to the community that is being served. And local authorities must be creative in their place-shaping: finding new ways to engage hard-to-reach groups, stimulating informed demand and diverse supply, unlocking the potential of the community and ensuring that local businesses and third sector organisations are part of a rich pattern of local provision.

We shall revise guidance in 2008 to reflect this demanding role and we will work with local authorities to help them meet the challenge of local leadership and provide the support they need.

7.16 The voluntary and community sector should be fully represented in the Children's Trust, just as it is vital that schools and other services close to children and their families are involved. We expect Children's Trusts to engage children and young people, a broad range of parental opinion, community interests, including faith communities, and local business.

7.17 It is the role of the Children's Trust to concert local action in the interests of better outcomes for children and young people, recognising that no one agency or interest can do that alone and that all have a common commitment to the wellbeing of children. To that end, the Children's Trust will consult widely, assess how well children in the locality are doing, prioritise and plan action, and commission services. Increasingly we expect the Children's Trust to look beyond direct local authority or other statutory service provision to a wide range of potential providers, in the voluntary and community sector and in the social enterprise and private sectors. Equally, we expect the Children's Trust regularly to evaluate results, to challenge where progress is slow, to listen to schools and other key delivery partners and to adjust and develop activities accordingly.

7.18 In many areas, Children's Trusts have developed rapidly since the launch of the Every Child Matters programme in 2003 and the Children Act 2004. Many Directors of Children's Services have shown outstanding leadership in seizing the agenda and drawing together local coalitions to drive improvements in children's services and children's wellbeing. It is right that arrangements have varied from area to area as there can be no fixed national blueprint for the development of local relationships. It is also the case, however, that the quality of relationships between agencies and the extent of involvement of key parties has varied from place to place. Going forward in the light of the Children's Plan, we expect greater consistency in the involvement of all relevant statutory agencies, the full involvement of the voluntary and community sector in the commissioning function and as providers, stronger mutual relationships between Children's Trusts and all schools and the fuller engagement of the wider community, including parents.

7.19 At the same time, it will be vital that national government, local authorities and their partners work together to strengthen Children's Trusts. We do not expect 150 Children's Trusts to find all the answers in isolation from one another. We will work with the Local Government Association, the NHS Confederation, the Association of Directors of Children's Services and with Chief Executives and others to understand better what works and to spread that learning. With Communities and Local Government and the Department of Health, the Department for Children, Schools and Families will support stronger local joint commissioning. And, with initiatives such as the joint Local Government Association/DCSF 'Narrowing the Gap' project, we will encourage the development of local authority-directed improvement programmes and capacity building.

7.20 Now that structures to support joined-up working are in place, we need to focus relentlessly on delivering measurable improvements for children and young people in every local area. **We expect local authorities and their strategic partners in Children's Trusts to champion and take responsibility for achieving measurable improvements in the lives of children** across all five Every Child Matters outcomes. We will use the new National Indicator Set, the NHS Outcomes Framework, Local Area Agreements and Comprehensive Area Assessments to provide sharper accountability for progress. Where performance falls short we will intervene quickly and work to identify areas for improvement.

7.21 To provide the basis for securing the improvements in outcomes, we will expect **Children's Trusts to have in place by 2010 consistent high quality arrangements to provide identification and early intervention for all children and young people who need additional help** in relation to their health, education, care and behaviour, including help for their parents as appropriate. These arrangements will be delivered through effective commissioning of services, including through private, voluntary and third sector providers, not by an old-style command and control approach.

7.22 To support this transformation, we will work with the Local Government Association and the Association of Directors of Children's Services to build capacity in the system. A new Centre for Excellence and Outcomes (CFEO) will begin work in July 2008, and a new programme to improve commissioning practice will be developed with local authority, health and voluntary sector partners to support Children's Trusts in building world class systems. The CFEO will review the evidence base for what works, and will work with local areas to apply this in their context.

7.23 Through these steps, we expect to strengthen the operation of Children's Trusts, looking in particular at the quality of partnerships at a local level and the extent to which trusts are accountable for all services for children. This includes reciprocal accountability to partners such as schools which are not bound by duties to co-operate. If a greater degree of consistent high quality is needed, **we will examine whether Children's Trust arrangements need to be strengthened, including by further legislation**.

7.24 These arrangements will also be strengthened by the new local government performance framework. The new performance framework provides more focused, but less bureaucratic accountability of local areas to central government and local people. However, the successful operation of this new performance framework for children's outcomes depends on each local provider being able to influence and hold its strategic partners to account for the contribution made to improving children's outcomes at a local level.

7.25 The new performance framework also signals a strong role for the local authority itself to drive improvement. Individual local authorities must build and sustain the effective partnership arrangements necessary to drive improvements in children's outcomes. Where this is not happening, there is a clear role for central government to help ensure that they do.

7.26 Local authorities and Children's Trusts also need to look beyond the services that work directly with children to all of those who make decisions that affect their lives, now and in the future. Decisions taken by transport, planning, housing and other local government services have direct and indirect consequences for the quality of children's and young people's lives, and all public services need to share a common responsibility for children's wellbeing.

7.27 In addition, the Children's Plan sets out our belief that we should be involving parents much more actively in shaping services around the needs of their children. We are committing to giving parents a stronger voice through a new DCSF Parents' Panel to comment on and review policy. One of the key responsibilities for Children's Trusts at a local level should be to ensure that they undertake high quality consultation on Children and Young People's Plans with parents, and engage parents actively on a more regular basis, to check on their progress and establish where services need to improve.

Accountability for success

7.28 As well as increasing expectations and accountability for joint working between services, we will also clarify the role of other partners:

- **Sure Start Children's Centres and other early years settings will be expected to work in partnership** across the private, voluntary, independent and maintained sectors and with primary schools, to drive up quality and ensure transitions are managed smoothly, with the quality of those partnerships assessed against measurable improvement. We want to see a stronger lead from local authorities in driving up the quality and consistency of early years provision across all sectors;

- **schools will have a new focus on progression and closing attainment gaps.** The best schools and teachers have always done this. We expect teachers to use tools for tracking pupil progress, assessment for learning and personal tutors to identify problems early, and the Common Assessment Framework where children may have significant needs that cannot be met in the classroom;

- **by 2010, all schools will be providing access to a range of extended services.** How these services look and are delivered in or through a particular school will vary and be shaped in consultation with parents, children and young people, but they will all offer a range of activities including study support and play, support for parents, including information sessions, family learning and more specialist support, swift and easy referral to specialist and targeted services, and wider community access to ICT, sports, adult learning and the arts;

- our programmes for renewing the fabric of our schools, Sure Start Children's Centres and other facilities must support co-location of services. We will **ensure that our capital investment programmes, including Building Schools for the Future, build in space for co-location of additional services, for play and community access, allow for joined up investment, and are linked with wider regeneration programmes**;

- the NHS provides universal support for all families, particularly when children are very young. The Children's Plan and the NHS Operating Framework signal a higher priority for children and young people in the operation of health services. **The new Child Health strategy will consider how health services can work better to improve children's health, working with schools and other partners**. We have established a review to consider how universal and specialist services, including Child and Adolescent Mental Health Services, can best work together to improve children's emotional wellbeing and mental health; and

- the police are an important partner in Children's Trusts, and increasingly involved with schools through Safer Schools Partnerships. The messages we received in the consultation about the importance of children and young people feeling safe, as well as our drive to reduce youth crime, underline the importance of the part the police can play.

7.29   To ensure that schools are being measured and rewarded for their contribution to children's overall wellbeing as well as to standards achieved, **we will develop strong school level indicators that taken together measure a school's contributions to pupil well-being**, using existing indicators (such as levels of attainment and progression, persistent absence and permanent exclusion, and proportion of children participating in PE and sport) and developing new ones, for example for bullying, obesity, entrance to the youth justice system, and destinations on leaving. **We will ask Ofsted to reflect these indicators in designing the cycle of inspections starting in 2009**. This will help strengthen the accountability of schools and of Children's Trusts. It will also provide clarity of expectation on schools that reflects their capacity and capability, and a better evidence base for the further development of Ofsted's risk-based approach to school inspection. We will also continue to work with the Implementation Review Unit, a group of school practitioners who provide scrutiny to policy development and implementation in the Department for Children, Schools and Families. We will, with their help, reinvigorate the New Relationship with Schools principles about effective, streamlined working between central government and schools.

7.30 We know that the wider wellbeing of children is essential to their attainment. **In early 2008 we will issue new guidance to schools on their duty to promote the wellbeing of their pupils.** This will further clarify how schools can promote all aspects of wellbeing for the pupils on their own roll and in their community through, for example, their ethos, curriculum, approach to behaviour and discipline, early intervention, engagement with parents, recruitment, extended provision and promotion of healthy eating and healthy lifestyles. We will consult schools, parents, children and young people about the minimum standards schools should meet to inform the guidance.

7.31 While schools' contribution to children's wellbeing is obviously extremely important, they can only succeed if other services also play their part. The Children's Plan has outlined how important maternity and other health services such as mental health services are to helping all parents and children including those particularly at risk. The engagement of the police in Safer Schools Partnerships has been a positive step in improving the links between schools and neighbourhood policing. Youth Offending Teams have a vital role to play in helping prevent youth crime and in protecting the community by preventing reoffending, and can only do their job effectively by having close contact with schools and local authorities. In evaluating the consistency of Children's Trust arrangements in all areas we will also be considering whether all services are playing their part and what might be done to break down barriers to better collaborative working where they exist.

The children's workforce

7.32 The quality of services for children and young people depends above all else on the people who work in them. The commitment and dedication of those who work with children has been at the heart of the improvement in children's lives we have seen over the last decade. However, the ambitions in the Children's Plan mean we need to continue to invest in the quality and capability of the children's workforce in all services and at all levels. In the preceding chapters, we set out specific measures for investing in specific workforces. In this chapter, we look at the workforce as a whole.

7.33 We want to build on the excellent practice that already exists at all levels to ensure consistent high quality services for children and families. We are seeking to ensure that members of the children's workforce are able easily to work together across professional boundaries to drive the full range of outcomes for every child. We are also looking to promote the active engagement of parents and the community as key partners in shaping and improving services for children.

> **Box 7.4: The children's workforce**
>
> The children's workforce comprises everyone who works with children, young people and families. This includes people working in settings like schools, Sure Start children's Centres and youth clubs as well as people working in health services, in social care and youth justice.
>
> Our vision for this workforce is of a team working on the basis of Every Child Matters. It is a workforce which understands Every Child Matters, its role in delivering Every Child Matters outcomes and its role in the team around the child.

7.34 Our vision is for a professional children's workforce that is graduate-led and, where appropriate, is qualified at least to Level 3 and reflects the diversity of the population.

7.35 We already have a graduate-led schools workforce, and have made good progress in developing Early Years Professionals and raising the general qualification level of the early years workforce. We are also working to professionalise the youth workforce. And as set out in Chapter 1, we will take action to drive up the quality of initial training and continuing professional development in social work, including piloting a newly qualified status from 2008/09 and establishing a professional development framework. We will also extend this approach to the play and the out-of-school childcare workforce.

7.36 To ensure we have the right structures to support the development and professionalisation of the workforce, we will re-examine the remits and scope of the organisations undertaking sector skills council, workforce reform and, in the longer term, regulatory roles. We will explore the scope for bringing within the remit of the Children's Workforce Development Council some groups that are currently supported by other sector skills councils to reinforce the concept of a single workforce. The Training and Development Agency, the National College for School Leadership and the Children's Workforce Development Council will work closely together to generate a stronger focus on integrated working.

Changing culture and practice

7.37 Building on this quality and capacity, we need to ensure that the children's workforce unites around a common purpose, language and identity, while keeping the strong and distinctive professional ethos of different practitioners in the workforce. We need also to ensure it has strong, effective and supportive leadership and management at all levels within the system, and that it is able to work comfortably in inter-agency and multi-disciplinary teams. Integrated working is pivotal to a personalised service that responds to individuals' needs in a seamless and timely manner.

7.38 **Further specific measures that will help us move towards our vision will be set out in the forthcoming Children's Workforce Action Plan, to be published in early 2008.**

7.39 The Children's Workforce Action Plan will set out in more detail our vision of integrated working, identifying the key workforce roles and our expectations of them. It will form a key part of the implementation of the Children's Plan by setting out measures that will:

- clarify and communicate the vision for integrated working, and the roles of settings, services and different groups of practitioners within it;

- support and challenge more effectively local areas to implement good practice models;

- engage universal services more effectively in identifying and assessing and acting on needs early and engaging targeted services; and

- drive workforce reform at all levels of the system, including embedding a culture of integrated working.

Integrated working

7.40 In practice, our vision means that practitioners need to work together as an integrated workforce, characterised by professional respect and trust, cutting across service boundaries to fit services around the needs of children, young people and families. This will involve working in teams made up of a range of people from different professional backgrounds.

7.41 This will be supported by a *Statement of Values for Integrated Working with Children and Young People* to be published in early 2008. This has been endorsed by the Children's Workforce Network as a resource for anyone working with children and young people. It is intended to capture the shared values that underpin the work of practitioners with distinct expertise and roles.

7.42 In many areas, groups of practitioners – for example school nurses, family support workers, learning mentors and others – are already working together as teams and with clusters of primary and secondary schools to provide effective early intervention, to support parents and to bring in more specialist help if needed. Often known as the 'team around the child', they sit alongside support for young children based in Children's Centres and targeted youth support teams for teenagers to provide seamless support for children, young people and families in an area. Where several practitioners are involved with a child, one will take on the role of lead professional, acting as the lead contact with services and working with the family helping to ensure that the support offered is coherent and focused on the needs of the child.

7.43 ContactPoint and eCAF (the electronic enablement of the Common Assessment Framework) are being developed to support integrated working. These systems serve different purposes but complement one another, and will be implemented nationally as a package. ContactPoint will allow authorised staff to find out quickly who else is working with the same child or young person, making it easier to make full assessments and deliver co-ordinated support. eCAF will be a single IT system available to all local authorities to support the Common Assessment Framework. It will allow practitioners electronically to create, store and share a CAF assessment securely and will promote a consistent approach that works across local authority and organisational boundaries.

7.44 Managers at all levels must support and promote integrated working, for example by leading the development and implementation of integrated services and common processes, and seeking opportunities for networking between colleagues from different backgrounds to develop and promote integrated working practices. They must also ensure that their staff are clear about their responsibilities and reporting lines, and that they get the continuing professional development they need to carry out their role.

7.45 Senior managers must lead on workforce reform and drive culture change to embed integrated working and common processes, communicating to their staff and to external stakeholders a clear vision of integrated working and how to achieve it, and allocating resources on the basis of need and local priorities and ensuring that performance management frameworks are joined up across services and support integrated working.

7.46 **We will publish a National Professional Development Framework for Leaders and Managers of Children's Services alongside the Children's Workforce Action Plan.** This will provide a basis for the professional development of leaders across all Children's Trust Partners.

Annex A: How we put the Children's Plan together

The national consultation process

A.1 The *Time to Talk* consultation was carried out using a number of strands during September and October 2007 and included children's focus groups, deliberative events, online and postcard responses and toolkits.

Focus groups and deliberative events

A.2 The main consultation events included focus groups of children and young people and a series of deliberative events held in four locations across the country with an invited list of young people aged 16 and over, parents, families and practitioners.

A.3 The focus groups were held with small groups of children and young people aged between 8 and 15 who were invited to respond to questions on themes central to the Children's Plan including staying safe, enjoying and achieving, families and communities. These groups met at different locations around the country and included a mix of girls and boys with different ethnic backgrounds.

A.4 The deliberative events were held in Birmingham, Leeds, London and Portsmouth and involved approximately 100 people at each venue, comprising:

- 30 parents of children and young people, with balanced representation from parents of children aged 0–7, 8–13 and 14–19;
- 30 young people aged 16–19; and
- 40 practitioners and policy experts, working with children of all ages.

A.5 The audience was balanced between the genders, and 15 per cent of the audience were from black and minority ethnic groups. Among the parents and young people were participants from the following groups:

- young offenders;
- children in foster homes or care homes;
- young people with learning disabilities;
- young people who are or have been home educated; and
- parents of children and young people who are home educated.

A.6   These events were followed up with invitations to organisations to run their own *Time to Talk* consultations using a toolkit.

Other consultation activity

A.7   The *Time to Talk* consultation included a leaflet-based and online questionnaire to capture views. The Department for Children, Schools and Families (DCSF) hosted a roadshow involving nine schools (one in each government region), reaching 462 children and young people to capture their input via a 'Big Brother' style diary room.

A.8   The DCSF worked with a range of stakeholders to ensure the consultation reached the widest range of audiences. We wrote to 300 key stakeholders in advance of the launch and during the consultation period and asked them to respond online, run their own consultations and encourage others they work with to do the same. In particular, we identified stakeholders who represent groups that do not usually take part in government consultations.

Summary of responses

A.9   The consultation received responses from 540 young people and 2,641 adults including representatives from public, private and voluntary sector bodies. More than 400 citizens participated in consultation events in Bristol, Leeds, London, Birmingham and Portsmouth.

Informing the Children's Plan

A.10   The results of the public consultation were reported back to the DCSF and were used to inform the Expert Group discussions and to develop the evidence report *Children and Young People Today: Evidence to support the development of the Children's Plan*. The *Time to Talk* consultation report and the evidence report can be read at www.dcsf.gov.uk/timetotalk.

Continued engagement after publication

A.11   The publication of the Children's Plan is not the end of the process and there will be continued activity to make sure that members of the public and stakeholders can continue to feed in their views. This is planned to include:

- further regional events early in 2008;

- sustaining the *Time to Talk* website as a place to post updates; and

- a range of other activities to keep testing out the Children's Plan, explaining its key messages and inviting views on what it means for different audiences.

The Expert Groups

A.12   As part of the consultation process and development of the Children's Plan, three Expert Groups were established by the Secretary of State for Children, Schools and Families in summer 2007. They were set up across three age ranges – 0–7, 8–13 and 14–19 – to look at the issues facing children, young people and their parents, and to make recommendations to the Secretary of State on how best to deliver his long-term objectives.

Membership and terms of reference

A.13 Group membership was drawn up to include representation across a range of professional backgrounds and organisations, including organisations working with disabled children and young people. Every effort was taken to ensure that there was an ethnic, gender and geographical balance, while also achieving a mix of professions across the groups.

A.14 The groups were chaired jointly by Ministers and leading external professionals:

0–7 group:

- Jo Davidson, Group Director of Children and Young People's Services for Gloucestershire County Council; and
- Rt Hon Beverley Hughes MP, Minister of State for Children, Young People and Families.

8–13 group:

- Sir Alan Steer, Headteacher, Seven Kings High School, London Borough of Redbridge;
- Lord Andrew Adonis, Parliamentary Under Secretary of State for Schools and Learners; and
- Kevin Brennan MP, Parliamentary Under Secretary of State for Children, Young People and Families.

14–19 group:

- Jackie Fisher, Chief Executive and Principal, Newcastle College; and
- Jim Knight MP, Minister of State for Schools and Learners.

A.15 The groups were asked to draw on evidence, research and views from delivery partners and children, parents and families and to use four central themes to organise their ideas:

- positive childhood;
- parents and families;
- personalisation; and
- prevention.

A.16 The groups met four times between September and November 2007. At their first meetings they prioritised the issues for debate. At the second meetings they debated in more depth the issues identified at the first, informed by early feedback from the *Time to Talk* consultation. The third meetings focused on developing the main points of the report. Members across all three Expert Groups met together at the fourth meeting to identify points they collectively wished to emphasise.

Informing the Children's Plan

A.17 The three Expert Groups each produced a report setting out a summary of their discussions and their recommendations. These reports were presented to the Secretary of State during the development of the Children's Plan and informed the Government's thinking on the proposals which are now set out in the Plan. The reports can be seen at www.dcsf.gov.uk/timetotalk.

Continued engagement after publication

A.18 The Expert Groups will continue their work beyond the publication of the Children's Plan and will support the Government in assessing progress against the commitments made in the Plan.

Annex B: The Children's Plan and the UNCRC

B.1 Since ratification of the United Nations Committee on the Rights of the Child (UNCRC) in 1991, the Government has pursued implementation through amendments to statute law, such as the amendments to the Children Act 1989, free standing legislation, in particular the Human Rights Act 1998, and through non legislative means. The latter includes key government programmes, in particular Every Child Matters, the Ten Year Youth Strategy and Every Parent Matters. These programmes, increasingly underpinned by the views of those they concern the most, are steadily improving outcomes for all children and thus the fuller realisation of their UNCRC rights. The appointment of the Children's Commissioner for England in 2005, who has specific responsibility for promoting the views and interests of children relating to the Every Child Matters outcomes, and who must regard to the UNCRC, is a further means, independent of Government, to promote children's outcomes and convention rights.

B.2 Our vision and ambitions set out in the Children's Plan reflect, and are informed by, both the General Principles and the Articles of the UNCRC. The content of each chapter relates to the clusters of Articles of the UNCRC and takes forward the recommendations of the UN Committee. As with the UNCRC, this Children's Plan reflects the holistic perspective of children's rights and outcomes that together will improve the lives and outcomes for children and young people.

UNCRC article clusters	Examples of linked key areas of the Children's Plan
The General Principles – the right to life and healthy development (article 6), the best interests of the child (article 3), the right to form and express their views (article 12) and the right to be protected from all forms of discrimination (article 2) – underpins the Plan and its development.	These are the very basics of the entire Children's Plan, together with the policies and initiatives set out within it.
Civil Rights and Freedoms: This cluster of articles sets out basic rights and freedoms for children in terms of their identity and information, for example: freedom of expression (article 13), right to access appropriate information (article 17) and the right not to be subjected to inhumane or degrading treatment or punishment (article 37a).	Chapter 2 sets out a series of actions to improve children and young people's safety, including publication of the Staying Safe Action Plan due to be published in 2008. This is underpinned by the recently announced Public Service Agreement to improve children's safety (PSA 13) and will build on legislation, policies and structures to make children safer that we have introduced over the past few years. Chapter 6 sets out proposals to improve information available to young people including how best to harness new technology.
Family environment and alternative care: This cluster of articles builds very much on the consideration of the child's best interests (article 3) and parental responsibility (article 18) and how governments can support both, ensuring that the rights and responsibilities of families are respected (article 5) and children are only separated from their families if it is in their best interests (article 9). It includes the rights for those children that do need to be separated from their birth families either through being looked after or adopted (articles 20, 21 and 25). Finally, the cluster includes the right for children to be protected from all forms of violence (article 19) and support for those children that have been victims of abuse or neglect (article 39).	Chapter 1 sets out proposals to improve wellbeing of children during and after family breakdown, children in care and on the edge of care, young carers and children going through the adoption process. Chapter 2 sets out actions to be taken to keep all children safe from harm and abuse. Chapter 3 outlines targeted intervention for vulnerable groups including effective outreach and intensive family support.

UNCRC article clusters	Examples of linked key areas of the Children's Plan
Basic Health & Welfare: The right to good quality health care (article 24) and support from the Government for maintaining a standard of living (article 27) are central to this cluster of articles. As well as ensuring adequate and appropriate support for children with mental health needs and disabled children (article 23), it includes the support the Government can provide for working parents (article 18(3)). Finally, it includes the financial support from the Government for families in need (article 26).	Chapter 1 sets out a range of policies to ensure that young people are healthy and enjoying life. Expanding provision of high quality childcare and more early years provision for 2-year-olds is set out in Chapters 3 and 4. Chapter 6 sets out actions to manage behaviour that puts young people at risk, including substance misuse and alcohol consumption, and to improve behaviour in the community.
Education, Leisure & Cultural activities: This cluster sets out the child's basic right to education (article 28) and governments' role in ensuring every child reaches their full potential (article 29). It also includes the child's right to play (article 31).	Chapter 1 sets out our plans for promoting an active childhood and highlights the importance of places to play. Chapters 3 and 4 set out our universal offer of support for personal and educational development together with how we will achieve our ambition of a world class workforce. Our proposals for 14–19-year-olds set out in Chapter 5 include personalised guidance and support and reforming the system of qualifications for 14–19-year-olds.
Special Protection Measures: The final cluster includes the child's right to protection from drug abuse (article 33), sexual abuse (article 34), trafficking (article 35) and all forms of exploitation (article 36). It includes the right for children who break the law to be treated humanely (article 37) and the use of imprisonment as a last resort (article 40).	The *Staying Safe Action Plan* due to be published in 2008 (set out in Chapter 2) will cover a full range of work to be taken forward to improve children's safety. Chapter 6 sets out proposals to prevent youth crime, improve outcomes for young offenders and reduce recidivism.

Annex C: Next steps

Introduction: Our ambition and the challenge

C.1   This document sets out our vision and ambitions for children and young people. We want every child to have a happy, healthy and safe childhood, and to develop into adults equipped with the breadth of skills, qualifications and experiences needed to be able to thrive in society and in the workforce. This annex sets out the further work that will be undertaken over the next year to make a reality of our vision and ambition.

How we will get there

C.2   As we set out our plans for implementation, we will respect procedures for assessing and funding new burdens on local authorities, and for carrying out impact assessments (to look at the costs and benefits of policies), together with other assessments such as equality and sustainable development.

Promoting the wellbeing and health of children and young people

C.3   Our vision for the next decade is one in which all children experience a healthy, happy childhood. In order to move towards this aim we will:

- publish a Child Health Strategy, jointly between Department of Health and Department for Children, Schools and Families;

- publish an Obesity Action Plan;

- undertake a major review of Child and Adolescent Mental Health Services; and

- publish a national play strategy.

Safeguard the young and vulnerable

C.4   To continue to make progress on safeguarding the young and vulnerable, we will:

- publish a response to the *Staying Safe* consultation and an action plan;

- publish the Byron Review on children and new technology, led by Dr Tanya Byron; and

- publish an independent assessment of the impact of commercial activity on children.

Achieve world class standards in education and close the gap in educational achievement for children from disadvantaged families

C.5   To achieve our aim of developing a world class education system in which all can achieve, we will now:

- consult on the right way to achieve our vision for parental engagement in secondary schools;

- evaluate the pilot of single level tests;

- review the Primary Curriculum, under the leadership of Sir Jim Rose;

- review progress on special educational needs provision by Her Majesty's Chief Inspector of Schools;

- publish the Bercow Review on speech and language therapy, led by John Bercow MP; and

- review implementation of the Steer report on behaviour, by Sir Alan Steer.

Ensure young people are participating and achieving their potential to 18 and beyond

C.6   To ensure that all young people have the opportunity to participate, we will:

- establish the independent regulator; and

- consult on the transfer of 16–19 funding from the Learning and Skills Council to local authorities.

Keep children and young people on the path to success

C.7   To keep children and young people on the path to success we will:

- publish a Youth Task Force Action Plan;

- publish a new Ten Year Drug Strategy; and

- publish a Youth Crime Action Plan.

Vision for children's services

C.8   To deliver on our vision of a collaborative, early intervention children's services system, we will:

- publish a Children's Workforce Action Plan;

- develop strong school level indicators for all the Every Child Matters outcomes; and

- review the consistency of Children's Trusts across local authorities.

Consulting with our Expert Groups

C.9 We have invited the Expert Groups to continue to work with the Department for Children, Schools and Families to review progress and they will:

- comment on and revise the delivery agreements for our Public Service Agreements in light of the Children's Plan;

- comment on our 2020 goals; and

- review the progress we make against the Children's Plan.

Consulting with children, young people, parents and professionals

C.10 To ensure that Government aims and policies reflect the priorities of children, young people, families and communities and build on best practice, we will establish an ongoing dialogue and consultation with children, young people, parents and professionals.

Updating on our progress

C.11 To hold ourselves to account publicly for our work, we will publish a progress report on the Children's Plan in a year's time.

Annex D: The National Curriculum, Key Stage tests and Levels

D.1   The National Curriculum provides an entitlement to a number of areas of learning for all pupils in maintained schools regardless of background and ability. The main phases of education in England are set out below. Note that there is not an exact match between ages and Key Stages: pupils may complete Key Stages at an earlier or later age depending on their progress. Independent schools do not need to adhere to the National Curriculum or deliver Key Stage tests.

Early Years Foundation Stage (age 0–5)

D.2   The Early Years Foundation Stage (EYFS) is a comprehensive framework for the learning, development and care of children in the early years. It was published in March 2007 and will become statutory in September 2008. It replaces and builds upon the existing separate early years frameworks: the *National Standards for Day Care and Childminding*, the *Curriculum Guidance for the Foundation Stage*, and the *Birth to Three Matters Framework*. The EYFS will apply to all settings offering provision for children aged 0–5, including day nurseries, pre-schools, playgroups, childminders and maintained and independent schools, to ensure that children receive the same high quality experience whatever type of setting they attend. The EYFS removes the existing legal distinction between care and education to better reflect the distinctive nature of provision in the early years – for young children, care and learning happen together and are indivisible. The EYFS expects practitioners to meet the individual needs of all children in their care and to provide a diverse range of play-based activities tailored to support children's development.

D.3   The EYFS is deliberately not part of the National Curriculum, but creates a distinct, coherent phase for all children aged 0–5. It places an expectation on practitioners to support children's learning and development in the following six equally important areas: 1) personal, social and emotional development; 2) communication, language and literacy; 3) problem solving, reasoning and numeracy; 4) knowledge and understanding of the world; 5) creative development; and 6) physical development. Practitioners are expected to assess children's progress through observation. The EYFS Profile is a tool to summarise children's achievements at the end of the Foundation Stage.

Key Stages

D.4   The National Curriculum for Key Stages 1–4 has eight levels, through which children progress.

D.5   National Curriculum tests measure performance at Levels 3–5 at the end of Key Stage 2. Tests measure performance at Levels 3–8 (mathematics), 3–7 (science) and 4–8 (English) at the end of Key Stage 3. Performance above those Levels can be recognised through teacher assessment, including exceptional performance for pupils who are working above Level 8.

Key Stage 1 (age 5–7)

D.6   This covers Year 1 and Year 2 in primary schools, with pupils assessed at the end of Year 2 when most are 7 years old. The National Curriculum specifies learning across ten subjects such as history, art and information technology, but the three core subjects are English, mathematics and science. Pupils take tests in reading, writing and mathematics but these are used only to inform overall teacher assessments – test results are not reported or collected centrally. Level 2 is considered the 'expected level' for pupils by age 7 and most pupils achieve this.

Key Stage 2 (age 7–11)

D.7   This takes pupils from Year 3 to Year 6 up to the age of 11 which is usually the end of primary education: the following year most pupils in maintained schools move to secondary schools. Pupils study ten National Curriculum subjects and, at the end of the Key Stage, pupils are assessed by teachers and take tests in English, mathematics and science. There is an expectation that pupils will achieve Level 4 by the age of 11, and national targets have been set to increase the proportion of children reaching this level.

Key Stage 3 (age 11–14)

D.8   This covers the first three years of secondary schooling (Year 7 to Year 9). The Key Stage 3 National Curriculum covers 12 subjects, with teacher assessment and tests in English, mathematics and science, and teacher assessment in the other foundation subjects. Expected attainment is Key Stage Level 5 or 6 and national targets have been set for the proportion achieving at least Key Stage Level 5.

Key Stage 4 (age 14–16)

D.9   This covers the final period (Year 10 and 11) of compulsory schooling during which pupils are working towards a range of academic and vocational qualifications, partly assessed via coursework. Every young person has to study English, mathematics, science, ICT, citizenship and PE as part of the core National Curriculum. They must also study religious education, careers education, sex education and work-related learning, and they have access to four entitlement areas covering the arts, design and technology, languages and humanities. Most of the assessment is at the end of Year 11. The qualifications are set by various independent awarding bodies. The main qualification is the GCSE (which is graded G up to A and then A*) but there are also a very wide range of other qualifications which can be taken by this age group. Targets have been set for the proportion achieving five or more GCSEs at grades C or above. This achievement level or its equivalent is also known as Level 2 (Level 1 being the acquisition of basic skills equivalent to five or more GCSEs at grades G or above). The latest target is set for the proportion achieving five or more including English and mathematics at C or above.

Key Stage 5

D.10 After the age of 16 many, but not all, pupils stay on in full-time education. Those that do study a range of academic and vocational qualifications in schools and with other further education providers such as colleges. The main academic qualification taken after two years (mainly by 18-year-olds) is the A level; the AS level is similar but is equivalent to half an A level. Students may be working towards qualifications at Level 1, Level 2 or Level 3. Achievement of Level 3 entails gaining two or more A levels at any grade, or the equivalent in other qualifications.

Printed in the UK for The Stationery Office Limited
on behalf of the Controller of Her Majesty's Stationery Office
ID5715810   12/07

Printed on Paper containing 75% recycled fibre content minimum.